Sabzi

Also by Yasmin Khan

Ripe Figs: Recipes and Stories from the Eastern Mediterranean

Zaitoun: Recipes and Stories from the Palestinian Kitchen

The Saffron Tales: Recipes from the Persian Kitchen

Sabzi

Fresh Vegetarian Recipes for Every Day

YASMIN KHAN

PHOTOGRAPHY BY JONATHAN GREGSON

BLOOMSBURY PUBLISHING
LONDON • OXFORD • NEW YORK • NEW DELHI • SYDNEY

For Mitra, finally

Contents

The Main Event 144

Dreamy Desserts 200

Introduction

Sabzi سبزی noun
Meaning: Herbs or leafy greens
Origin: Persian

IF THERE IS one word that defines the food I love to eat, it's *sabzi* – the Persian word for fresh greens and herbs.

Sabzi in my home isn't a casual afterthought, a small sprinkling of chopped parsley to garnish a stew or a few sprigs of coriander to brighten a noodle soup. No, sabzi is the cornerstone of most of the meals I cook and the bedrock of so many khoreshts, curries, soups, salads, breakfasts, and sandwiches my mother prepared for us when I was growing up. Sabzi is the scent of my main cultural holiday – Nowruz, the Persian New Year – in which fresh greens take on a ritualistic, symbolic significance as we grow them in the weeks before the spring equinox and place them on our Nowruz altar to represent rebirth and renewal. If cinnamon, nutmeg, and cloves are the comforting and ambrosial scents of Christmas, then freshly chopped dill, ribbons of tarragon, pungent fenugreek leaves, and peppery stalks of chives are what transport me home.

From the plate of Thai basil (hung quế) and coriander (ngò gai) served alongside bowls of Vietnamese pho to the piles of finely chopped parsley and mint used to make Lebanese tabbouleh, many cuisines around the world embrace sabzi (even if they don't call it by that name). But I have yet to find a food culture that so enthusiastically and without abandon feasts on fresh herbs as Iranians do. In Persian cuisine, fresh sabzi is chopped into frittatas, minced into thick pastes that are then used to stuff chicken and fish, and simmered by the pound to make thick, hearty stews. Most days sabzi will be eaten simply and unadorned, by the handful, with fresh feta cheese, walnuts, and bread for breakfast or a snack.

Sabzi also means vegetables in Urdu, the language of my Pakistani father, and it is used in Pakistan to describe cooked vegetables. These include some of my favourite Punjabi dishes that I grew up on, from bindi, braised okra in a spicy masala, to kerala, pungent bitter melon sautéed with sweet onions, or my dad's favourite aloo matar gajar (potatoes, peas, and carrots) that we would scoop up enthusiastically with warm rotis.

All of which has meant that when the idea for a vegetarian cookbook first planted its seed in my mind (driven in part by the many requests that came in from my readers), I knew straight away that I would call it *Sabzi* and that it could be an opportunity to share the food I most often cook at home, which for a multitude of reasons – social, political, health, and economic – is primarily vegetable focused.

It also felt fitting, given that sabzi represents new beginnings in Iranian culture, that I wrote this book while embarking on a new chapter of my life – my journey to motherhood. While pregnant, I predominantly craved the Iranian food my maternal family cooked, perhaps not surprising, as these are the foods I most commonly associate with nurture. From mint and parsley celery stews that felt like clouds parting on a bright spring day, to sour cherry and saffron fragranced rice pilafs that looked as ornate as Persian carpet, and endless bowls of ruby red pomegranates that glistened and crunched, bringing a smile to my face and deep satisfaction to my ever-expanding belly.

As I thought about the meals I would cook for my daughter, the desire to share with her the culture and cuisine of my mixed heritage – Iranian and Pakistani – took on a greater significance and made me think about ancestry, lineage, and the power of our ancient traditions. I knew I wanted to pass on these food memories to my new family, but to do so in a way that was fresh and reflected our contemporary way of eating.

It felt, therefore, like an appropriate time to explore a different type of cookbook for me, one that focuses wholeheartedly on the ingredients and recipes I instinctively turn to – and away from the travel reportage that has driven my food writing so far. The food I cook in my North London flat is influenced by memories and stories from the many countries I've lived, worked, or travelled in over the course of my life. My kitchen is filled with the sweet scent of saffron, the sharp zest of lemons, and the brightness of fresh herbs – ingredients that define the meals I most commonly prepare. I've loved bringing these recipes together and am thrilled to invite you in, to share a more intimate slice of my life and the food I love.

I hope you'll join me in feasting on these recipes and come to agree that whatever is placed on the dining table, most meals can be improved with a big bowl of greens, or sabzi, on the side.

Yasmin X

£15.40 K.G

Eating the Rainbow

FOR AS LONG as I can remember, I have loved to eat. And vegetables just may be my first love.

Charred aubergine, sweet and smoky, pounded with garlic and pomegranate molasses. Sautéed chard, smothered in tahini and sprinkled with scarlet chilli flakes. Fresh broad beans, popped from their pods, simmered with dill and turmeric. Pumpkin, roasted with sugar and cinnamon, to accompany a cup of tea. Loving vegetables was easy when I was growing up, because the meals my family cooked firmly celebrated them.

Vegetables were also how my grandparents earned a living.

My mum's side of the family is from an agrarian region of northwest Iran, a lush province full of dense forests, sparkling rivers, and craggy mountains, with soil so fertile that almost half the land is used for agriculture. It's an area known for its tea plantations and rice paddies, and my grandparents had the latter, a small rice farm where they grew almost all the food they needed to be self-sufficient and enough to make a humble living selling produce in local markets.

Visiting my grandparents on holidays from England meant being uprooted from industrial and concrete inner-city Birmingham and replanted in an abundant, vibrant paradise. Salads of buttery lettuce, crunchy cucumbers, and sweet tomatoes came from the vegetable patch mere metres from the kitchen window. Hearty stews were made with pink and white speckled beans, newly popped from their pods, whole bulbs of fresh young garlic, and handfuls of herbs that my aunts sent us out to harvest from the land. Best of all, for me, was the abundance of fruit that grew all around us – pomegranates, quinces, and persimmons in the winter; strawberries, watermelons, and figs in the summer. Our milk and yoghurt were locally sourced, too, coming straight from the ten dairy cows that lived on my family's farm. My grandmother taught me how to milk my favourite cow, who I affectionately had named Parisa, and then hand-churn butter from this milk as we sat cross-legged on a woven Persian carpet on her kitchen floor.

If that all seems too idyllic, well, the reality was far from a fairy tale.

The fraught political situation in Iran in the 1980s and the Iran-Iraq war enveloped every aspect of my family's life and, as anyone who has been around small-scale agriculture will tell you, the life of a small-scale farmer is *hard*. It takes a huge amount of toil to grow crops from seed, to keep soil healthy, and to harvest produce in hot fields under a scorching sun. You live with a constant sense of precarity, your livelihood in the hands of elements you can't control. Too much rain – or too little – and your crop can be ruined, and along with it a whole year's income. Rigged global trade rules and cheap imports from multinational corporations push prices down and you can't compete. Soil erosion, plant

diseases, and the availability of seeds fluctuate each year, vastly affecting your yield. It wasn't hugely surprising, then, when one of my uncles took over the farm after my grandfather passed away and changed the focus of the farm from plants to livestock. This change reflects a more general shift in farming over the last few decades, as small-scale farming communities around the globe have been forced to change their traditional food-growing practices because of an unjust global food system that favours corporate profit over sustainability and human rights, as well as the ever-increasing extreme changes in weather patterns. Instead of growing fruits and vegetables for local consumption, as has been commonplace for most of human history, food production is increasingly dominated by cash crops and growing food that can compete with the demands of a global supply chain.

While the traditional method of how my family grew food has changed, the legacy of how they cooked and ate food continues to shape my eating habits. As does the influence of my mother, who when I was three months old, whisked me off to Iran as she finished her PhD fieldwork in nutrition and dietetics. Later, my mum worked as a community health professional before eventually becoming a professor of public health. The food I ate as a child was what you would imagine for someone whose mother's career was dominated by teaching people about healthy eating. Our meals were prepared with whole foods and whole grains. We snacked on dried fruits and nuts and picnicked on summer days with small boats of chilled romaine lettuce that we dunked into a herb-flecked sweet and sour Iranian vinegar dressing known as sekanjabeen.

When I was six years old, I remember my mum describing in intricate detail how most commercial sausages were made, what went in them and how the animals were kept, instilling in me a lifelong aversion to processed meat. She fed me every fruit and vegetable under the rainbow that she could afford, not an easy feat back then, having only recently arrived in the UK as a new immigrant and subsisting on a very low wage. She cooked from scratch every day, making us healthy, homemade meals despite working a demanding job – something, as I've got older, I've marvelled at – and taught me to truly enjoy the food I eat. No food was ever forbidden either – be it deep-fried or drenched in sugar – but I learned that such treats were something to be savoured on special occasions, and that nothing needed to be off-limits in a varied and balanced diet.

She also taught me, through the endless stream of guests we had to stay at our family home and through the regular, and often raucous, parties that my parents would throw, feeding 20 or 30 people, that eating communally could do more to nourish body and soul than being overly dogmatic about the specific nutritional content of a meal. This, perhaps, has been the biggest legacy of my childhood eating: the idea that gathering to share food with others is one of the most life-giving acts you can undertake.

My mum's influence in feeding me a colourful diet, packed with fruits and vegetables, has meant that for most of my adult life, even though I am an omnivore, the food I cook at home has always put fresh plants at the heart of what I eat. But this is cultural, too, and extends beyond just the influence of my immediate family.

One of the cornerstones of the Iranian way of eating is the enthusiastic enjoyment of fruits, vegetables, nuts, and beans as savoury snacks. It includes the ritual of eating sour fruits such as pomegranates, sour cherries, and kiwis sprinkled with salt and golpar, a citrusy and slightly bitter ground spice that complements the acidity of sharper fruits and aids their digestion. Golpar is also combined with salt and vinegar to sprinkle over boiled whole broad beans, which are enjoyed in a thoroughly sensory way, eaten with your hands, using your fingers and teeth to pop open their thick shells before popping the soft bean into your mouth. In the autumn and winter months, vegetables such as beetroots and pumpkins are steamed long and slow, with just a little sugar, to bring out their sweetness and intensify their flavours, and in the summer, dalaar is spread over unripe green plums or crunchy cucumber. Nuts and seeds are given special treatment too – with pistachios, almonds, chickpeas, and cashews roasted with lemon, saffron, and salt to make a savoury nut mix called ajil. Bowls of melon, squash, and pumpkin seeds are toasted with the same sour, fragrant, and salty base and are

ORGANIC
POLISH ROSE
TOMATOES
£8.80/KG
ITALIAN
CAMONE TOMATO
£9.90 /kg
SPANISH
BLACK TOMATOES
£6.60 /kg

present in nearly every Iranian's home. Growing up with all of these delicious treats made it easy to incorporate plant-based snacks into my everyday eating.

Later, as I worked for NGOs in the global justice movement and learned about the health and environmental impact of industrially farmed food products, I became more committed to this way of eating, focusing on sourcing organic produce from good suppliers whenever I could. This immediately and quite dramatically reduced the amount of meat that I could afford, and so the food I cooked at home shifted accordingly. Later still, when I was putting together the proposal for my first book, *The Saffron Tales*, I took a job managing the pioneering health charity Made in Hackney, which ran food growing and cooking classes promoting local, seasonal, plant-based food to low-income and disadvantaged groups in London. Through my time at the charity I learned a whole host of new ways to cook delicious vegan food. These days, while I still enjoy cooking and eating meat and fish, it feels like a treat, which perhaps is how it should be, not only for our health but also for the health of our planet.

So in this book are dishes that showcase the vegetarian meals I most commonly prepare at home. Most of the recipes are influenced by the cuisines of my parents' heritage – Pakistani and Iranian – but I have also included recipes inspired by my travels around the world. I have a habit of returning from each place I visit with a fun set of ingredients or kitchen accessories to play with. A six-month stint in Latin America saw me come home with an arepa maker, huge bags of masa harina, and a newfound addiction to smoky black bean stews. A family holiday to Morocco introduced me to the enchanting world of fruit-, nut-, and cinnamon-spiked tagines, which I remember every time I lay out the colourful, geometric-patterned mezze plates I brought back from the markets of Marrakesh. A year living in Thailand left me addicted to coconut-enriched tofu curries, which are now part of my regular weeknight dinner rotation. While the recipes in this book reflect the Mediterranean and Middle Eastern techniques and ingredients I know best, they also recreate flavours I have loved from all over the world, interpreted through my personal lens and by no means authentic – though I hope you'll agree that they are delicious.

My journey to motherhood was long, twisted, and arduous and led to me making the conscious decision to spend less time on the road, putting down, for now at least, my love of travel and foreign adventures. But it came with its own rewards and led to a desire to spend more time in my kitchen, recreating favourite dishes from places I've visited and adapting them by making them vegetable-centred. This time in the kitchen was also influenced by my marriage to a fellow writer who has been vegetarian since he was 12 years old. In a desire to share the food of my ancestry with him, I began recreating the classic Iranian dishes I grew up with, omitting the meat and fish. I found it frustrating at first and, truth be told, wondered how I would be able to share my culture with him if I couldn't share my food. But it proved a helpful lesson, as it made me realise that if we are collectively, as a global community, to transition to a more ecological and just food system to deal with the magnitude of the climate crisis, we will have to grapple with something far more difficult than simply reducing the number of

burgers we eat. We'll have to resculpt our deeply embedded emotional attachment to the dishes we grew up with and the family meals that we associate with our sense of belonging, our history, and our heritage. I'm talking about the roast dinners we ate at Sunday lunchtime, the cookouts for the Fourth of July, the lamb biryanis feasted on at Eid, and the turkey we tucked into at Thanksgiving and Christmas. Creating new food pathways to honour our cultural traditions is an important part of the transition to eating less meat and dairy. This is why it has felt important in this book to share plant-based versions of the traditional Iranian dishes I grew up eating, so those of us who want to reduce our carbon footprint, or simply eat more healthily, can still be swept away by the aromatics of slow-cooked herbs or the sharpness of dried limes, enabling us to carry on our traditions with future generations.

What follows in these pages, then, is a celebration of my favourite vegetable dishes, inspired by my travels but rooted in how I cook at home. I hope the recipes nourish and comfort you as much as they do me – and help you fall a little more in love with vegetables, too.

My Cupboard Essentials

THE FOOD I buy and eat is influenced by where I live, in a pocket of London dominated by Turkish greengrocers, which, handily for me, stock all the ingredients I need to cook the Middle Eastern and Mediterranean food I so adore.

The increased popularity of these ingredients has meant that most larger supermarkets and health food stores also now stock products such as tahini, pomegranate molasses, za'atar, dried limes, and the delightfully fragrant mild chilli flakes known as Aleppo pepper. The following lists are the key ingredients in my cooking that you may want to stock up on for making the recipes in this book. I welcome you to embrace them and experiment in your cooking beyond my recipes, too.

Being of mixed heritage, I've always felt comfortable melding influences when it comes to food (and indeed to all culture), so I don't think there should be any rules in bringing together ingredients – apart from the rule that it has to taste good. Investing in these ingredients will give you a well-stocked pantry as you decide what to make from this book, and then you can simply choose your vegetables and fresh herbs according to the season or your mood.

A quick note on substitutions: Most of the recipes in this book are dairy- and egg-free, so they are suitable for people on a wide variety of diets. Many of the remaining recipes can be easily adapted to use plant-based ingredients such as olive oil instead of butter, a nut milk instead of cow's milk, or a vegan alternative to feta, Parmesan, or Greek-style yoghurt. The way I cook is often flexible in this way, depending on who I'm eating with or if I want a lighter meal. The one exception is the baking recipes, which do need to be followed with the ingredients listed in order to work.

OILS AND CONDIMENTS

Extra-virgin olive oil
Vegetable oil
Apple cider vinegar
Pomegranate molasses
Soy sauce or tamari
Vegan or traditional oyster sauce
Vegan or traditional fish sauce
Vegan or traditional Worcestershire sauce
Chilli oils
Dijon mustard
Honey
Maple syrup
Tahini

DRIED SPICES AND HERBS

Za'atar
Aleppo pepper or other mild chilli flakes
Saffron
Dried limes
Dried mint
Dried oregano
Paprika – sweet, smoked, and hot
Ground turmeric
Cumin – ground and whole seeds
Coriander – ground and whole seeds
Ground cinnamon
Ground nutmeg
Ground allspice
Garam masala
Curry powder
Brown and yellow mustard seeds
Dried curry leaves
Fenugreek leaves (kasoori methi)
Good quality vegetable bouillon powder

GRAINS AND PULSES

Basmati rice – white and brown
Bulgar wheat
Dried pasta
Red, Puy, and green or brown lentils
Mung beans – whole and split

NUTS AND SEEDS

Walnuts
Pistachios
Almonds
Pine nuts
Pumpkin seeds
Flax seed/linseed
Sunflower seeds

TINNED OR JARRED

Red kidney beans
Chickpeas
White beans
Pinto beans
Tomatoes
Tomato purée
Coconut milk

FRESH

Lemons
Limes
Onions
Garlic

CHILLED

Feta cheese
Natural yoghurt – full-fat Greek-style or plant-based
Tofu – silken and firm
Tempeh
Parmesan cheese
Eggs

Kitchen Hacks

How to Get the Most from Your Ingredients

HERE ARE SOME suggestions for how you might approach cooking the recipes in this book, as well as a few tips and tricks that have helped me become a better cook over the years.

When planning a meal, think about how to balance textures, temperatures, and acidity.

Iranian food culture places this premise at the heart of every meal, and it's a technique I try to incorporate whenever I am cooking. A rich Persian khoresht, for example, served with rice, will always need a fresh and crunchy side salad dressed in a sharp vinaigrette to cut through the richness of the stew, or some yoghurt to balance the heat of the main dish. A mezze is made magnificent through the careful balance of hot and cold plates, from the smoothness of a dip that you slide a piece of pitta bread through, to the chewy mouthfeel of a bulgar salad, and the heat and smoke imparted by the grill. Thinking ahead of time about how your meal will look, smell, taste, feel, and sound as you eat will elevate your cooking and can mean anything from the addition of some toasted seeds for crunch, a dash of sumac for sharpness, or a tangle of herbs for colour.

Prioritise umami.

One of the main differences I've found in focussing on vegetable-based cookery as opposed to preparing food with meat and fish is that flavours need to be layered more deliberately. For me, that often means thinking about how I might add umami. Over the years, this has led to a habit of adding ingredients such as soy sauce, Marmite, Worcestershire sauce, and miso to dishes from cuisines where they are not often used but I feel might benefit from an extra layer of depth. Sauces, soups, and stocks can all benefit from these flavour enhancers, and I've found soy sauce in particular a handy way to add oomph to the many Persian stews that I've adapted to make plant-based.

Toast and grind your spices.

Toasting and grinding your own spices is truly worth the effort, and I've written the recipes in this book with freshly toasted spices in mind. Having said that, I know what it's like to need to quickly throw a meal together, and that toasting and grinding spices isn't always a top priority if you are short on time. So, my suggestion is to meet me somewhere in the middle. If you want to speed things up, batch-grind toasted spices on the weekend and use them when you are cooking. You don't need to do this for all your spices, but the basic ones that are often used in this book, such as cumin and coriander, are transformed by this step. I promise, it takes only 4 minutes to toast and grind. (I use a small spice grinder or coffee grinder if I'm working in batches, but you could use a mortar and pestle.) For shop-bought pre-ground spices, I recommend replacing them every 6 months. If that isn't an affordable option, simply add a bit more than the recipe suggests, as you'll probably find that the intensity of their flavour will dull over time.

Choose the right oils.

I wince when I see people fry food in fancy extra-virgin olive oil. It is such a waste of an expensive product. I have several bottles of oils on the go at the same time in my house. I stick to cheaper, lighter, neutral vegetable oils such as sunflower for frying, or a light olive oil. I then buy a medium-bodied extra-virgin olive oil for adding to soups or stews, and a really good-quality strong-bodied extra-virgin olive oil that never goes anywhere near heat and is used for dressings or a final drizzle on a dish.

Taste your food throughout the cooking process and season at the beginning, in the middle, and at the end.

The key to good cooking is understanding your palate and learning tweaks to mould dishes to your taste. You'll never get that through a recipe – it's all through practise and about getting familiar with the food you cook. Taste is personal, so what works for me might not work for you. The key is to build your confidence and identify your preferences, and the best way to do that is to taste throughout the cooking process. And don't forget that seasoning isn't just about salt and pepper – lemon juice, soy sauce, chilli flakes, and olive oil are excellent flavour enhancers too.

Cook beans from scratch, when you can.

Cooking beans and pulses from scratch is not only more affordable, but it also gives them a better flavour and texture. Like most people, I rely on tinned or jarred beans midweek, but if I have a bit more time on the weekend, I try to cook up big batches of beans or lentils that I can then use during the week (or freeze for when I need them). Here is my rough guide:

- Rinse 300g dried beans in cold water, then put them in a big bowl of water. Add 2 teaspoons salt and a strip of kombu seaweed to the water. This softens the beans, making them creamier, and the enzymes in the kombu help break down the beans and make them more digestible. Kombu can be expensive to source, but you don't need much of it – a 7.5cm square will do.
- Let the beans soak for 8 hours or overnight – soaking is crucial as it helps release some of the chemical components that can make beans hard to digest. If I know I want to cook beans that evening, I often put a bowl to soak while I'm having breakfast in the morning and then come back to it after work.
- When it's time to cook the beans, rinse and drain them and transfer to a large

saucepan. Top with enough water to cover them by around 5cm. Bring to a rolling boil for 5 minutes, using a spoon to remove any grey scum that rises to the surface. Turn the heat down to a simmer, cover, and cook the beans until they are soft. After 20 minutes, add 1 teaspoon salt. If it starts looking a bit dry, top with some more water – different beans will absorb different amounts.

- How long it will take to cook the beans will vary depending on their age and quality, anywhere from 45 minutes to 1½ hours. Soaking for 8 hours helps even this out, but it still can be a little unpredictable. Your best bet is to find a supplier you like and cook with their beans a few times until you work out their most common cooking times. I always give a range of timings and encourage you to follow your instincts. If the beans are soft enough to pinch together between your thumb and forefinger, they are done.
- Sometimes beans will be too old to properly cook, and no amount of cooking time will get them there. It's infuriating when this happens, and it can be hard to rescue them. Just make a note not to buy that brand again.
- Beans and lentils flourish with two ingredients: lots of fat and lots of salt. Be generous with both and you will be rewarded.
- A good rule of thumb is that beans will roughly double in volume and weight when they cook. Of course, this will vary by bean variety. It's a trial-and-error process to work out which of your beans will cook a certain way, but it does no harm to cook extra if you aren't sure, as they keep well for a few days and can be added to soups, salads, and stews or puréed with some garlic, lemon, and extra-virgin olive oil for a tasty dip.

Menu Planning

Quick and Easy

My Favourite Mezze

Worth That Extra Bit of Effort

Best for Batch-Cooking and Freezing

Picnics and BBQs

Lighter Meals

Bountiful Breakfasts

Eat your breakfast yourself, share your lunch with a friend, and give your dinner to your enemy.

– **MIDDLE EASTERN PROVERB**

Breakfasts are a serious affair in my family. A trip to visit my relatives often involves sitting down to a lavish Iranian spread of toasted flatbreads, sheep's and goat's cheeses, sweet jams, sticky honey, fresh fruit, sliced tomatoes and cucumbers, walnuts, fried or boiled eggs, and, because we simply cannot imagine any serious meal without it, a platter of fresh herbs.

My weekday breakfasts tend to be less elaborate, but I still like to prioritise quick and creative ways to spruce up my regular rotation of eggs with toasted bread, porridge, fruit with yoghurt, and beans on toast. The following breakfasts are a mix of sweet and savoury, light and hearty, warm and cold, all relatively easy to make and packed with flavour to hopefully inspire you to add some twists to what you regularly eat in the mornings. From homemade granolas to spiced masala omelettes and smoky tofu scrambles, there is something for everyone who likes to start their day with a nourishing meal.

Treats on Toast

When I get asked about the food I eat the most, the answer is inevitably "things on toast". This is partly out of laziness, but also because I always have a few loaves of bread in my freezer. Often when I'm in need of a snack, I simply open the fridge and pile whatever I can find in there on toasted bread. Here are a few of my favourite combinations born out of those fridge raids (see the photo on page 35). A really good-quality extra-virgin olive oil will make all these taste so much better, so invest in the best you can afford.

Hummus, Tomato, and Sauerkraut

If you need a reset breakfast after a night of indulging, this is for you. I love the tangy, sour crunch of the sauerkraut mixed with sweet, juicy tomatoes and smooth, garlicky hummus. Simply spread a thick layer of hummus on toasted bread, top with slices of tomato, sprinkle with salt, add a generous pile of sauerkraut, drizzle with extra-virgin olive oil, and finish with freshly ground black pepper.

Labneh, Fried Egg, and Za'atar

This hearty concoction reminds me of meals I have enjoyed in Palestine, where bread, labneh, eggs, and za'atar are commonly served at breakfast. For each piece of toast, season 50g labneh (or thick, strained Greek-style yoghurt with a pinch of salt) with a tiny bit of crushed garlic or a pinch of garlic granules. Then, fry an egg sunny-side up and let it sit on a plate lined with kitchen paper to soak up the excess oil. To assemble, spread the garlicky yoghurt over the toasted bread, top with the egg, sprinkle with salt, and finish with a good-quality za'atar spice mix.

Halloumi, Apricot Jam, and Mint

The island of Cyprus introduced me to the wide, wonderful range of halloumi dishes, and pairing it with apricot and mint results in a winning sweet-salty combination, one of my favourite ways to enjoy the world's best squeaky cheese. Begin by frying a couple of slices of halloumi until golden brown on each side, then transfer to a plate lined with kitchen paper. While the halloumi is cooking, toast and butter your bread, then spread with apricot jam. Top with the slices of fried halloumi and finish with finely chopped mint leaves.

Avocado, Tomato, and Za'atar

I know it's much scorned, but the millennial in me is still a big fan of avo toast in all its forms. To make it for one person, mash half an avocado in a small bowl with a generous pinch of salt, freshly ground black pepper, and a squeeze of lemon. Spread on toast and top with slices of sweet tomato, a liberal smattering of za'atar, and plenty of top-quality extra-virgin olive oil.

Cheddar, Rocket, and Lime Achaar

A few years back, there was a restaurant near where I live in East London called the Raw Duck, which as part of their Sunday brunch served buttered crumpets topped with slices of Cheddar and an Indian subcontinent-style lime pickle on top. The flavour combination was wild. I often return to it for a savoury start to the day. Simply butter your toast (or crumpet!), layer over a small amount of rocket leaves, add thick slices of extra mature Cheddar cheese, and dot small pieces of lime pickle or other achaar over it.

Ricotta, Fresh Figs, and Honey

I'm forever beholden to the scent and sweetness of a perfectly ripe fig, which reminds me of holidays in the Mediterranean. This Italian-inspired combination of thick, creamy, cold ricotta, spread thickly over toasted bread and topped with sliced ripe figs and a drizzle of honey takes me back to the hills of Tuscany, which, let's be honest, is one of the best places to be transported to with a simple bite of breakfast.

Middle Eastern Breakfast Platter

I eat a variation of this Middle Eastern breakfast platter whenever I gather with my family for weekend brunches. We always have the Iranian essentials (feta, walnuts, fresh herbs, flatbreads) but often supplement with Levantine additions such as avocados, labneh, and za'atar. There are no specific measurements; just assemble a big sharing spread using whatever you have in the kitchen and what your personal preferences are. The fresh herbs are a must though!

ESSENTIALS

Big handfuls of mixed herbs (coriander, tarragon, basil, chives, mint, parsley)

A block of feta cheese

Walnuts

Slices of tomato and cucumber

Crunchy radishes

Hard-boiled eggs, peeled and halved

Salted gherkins

Butter

Honey

Fruit jams

Flatbreads

Fragrant black tea, such as Darjeeling or Earl Grey

OPTIONAL EXTRAS

Slices of avocado tossed with extra-virgin olive oil, lemon juice, Aleppo pepper or other mild chilli flakes, salt, and freshly ground black pepper

Labneh drizzled with extra-virgin olive oil and za'atar

Maple Granola
with Fruit and Kefir Yoghurt

SERVES ABOUT 8

GRANOLA

80ml melted coconut oil or vegetable oil
120ml maple syrup (or 80ml if you don't want it too sweet and are adding dried fruit)
2 large egg whites (optional)
1 teaspoon vanilla extract
1 teaspoon ground cinnamon
350g jumbo rolled oats
3 tablespoons milled flax seeds
50g sunflower seeds
50g pumpkin seeds
50g flaked almonds, coconut flakes, or chopped pistachios
50g dried fruit, such as cherries or raisins (optional)
Salt

ACCOMPANIMENTS

Kefir
Greek-style yoghurt
Seasonal fruit

Seasonal fruit served with kefir-spiked yoghurt and a crunchy, seeded granola is my go-to summer breakfast, a throwback to when I used to work at a wellness resort in the Gulf of Thailand. You can use whatever fruit you like for this breakfast, and making your own granola is a game changer. It's so much more affordable and healthier than the shop-bought stuff, which is laden with sugar and often eye-wateringly expensive. The addition of egg white is optional, but it does help bind the granola. The granola keeps well in an airtight container at room temperature for about 3 weeks. I often buy kefir as a drinking yoghurt and mix it into a Greek-style yoghurt, so I get an extra probiotic hit in the morning.

Preheat the oven to 150°C/Fan 130°C/Gas Mark 2. Line a large baking sheet with baking paper.

In a large bowl, combine the oil, maple syrup, egg whites (if using), vanilla, cinnamon, and ¼ teaspoon salt and whisk until frothy. Stir in the oats, flax seeds, sunflower seeds, pumpkin seeds, and almonds and mix well.

Transfer the granola to the prepared baking sheet and spread in an even layer. You don't need to spread it out too thinly, as you need the grains and nuts to be touching in order for them to clump together. Bake for 30 minutes or until it looks golden brown and crunchy, turning the baking sheet halfway through cooking to ensure the granola cooks evenly. Remove from the oven and let cool. Once cooled, you can mix in any dried fruit if you are using it, and transfer to a jar.

When ready to serve, whisk some kefir into a dollop of yoghurt. Serve the fruit in bowls, topped with the kefir yoghurt and granola.

Overnight Oats
with Pomegranates and Pistachios

SERVES 2

OVERNIGHT OATS

100g jumbo rolled oats

1 apple or pear, cored and grated

240ml water

200g full-fat yoghurt or plant-based yoghurt

2 teaspoons runny honey or maple syrup

¼ teaspoon ground cinnamon

2 to 4 tablespoons kefir (optional)

2 tablespoons milled flax seeds

Salt

TOPPINGS

Pistachios, roughly chopped

Pumpkin seeds

Pomegranate seeds or seasonal fruit of choice

Honey

Short on time in the morning? It takes just minutes to prep this heavenly breakfast the night before, ready for you to enjoy with minimal effort in the morning. You can replace the pomegranate seeds with any seasonal fruit – berries, nectarines, and persimmons all work well. I prefer to stir in the ground flax seeds just before eating, but if you don't mind the oats taking on a thicker, more viscous quality, you can stir them in the night before. Adding a few tablespoons of kefir gives another probiotic hit, which will keep your gut happy. Sealed in a jar or container, or simply with a plate over your bowl, these oats will keep in the fridge for up to 2 days.

Combine the oats, apple, water, yoghurt, honey, cinnamon, and a pinch of salt in a container with a lid and stir well to ensure the oats are fully mixed into the liquids. Mix in the kefir, if using. Cover and transfer to the fridge for at least 10 hours.

When you are ready to eat, stir in the flax seeds, then spoon the oats into a bowl and add your favourite toppings and a drizzle of honey.

Masala Omelette

SERVES 1

2 or 3 large eggs
2 tablespoons whole milk or plant-based milk
½ teaspoon ground cumin
¼ teaspoon ground turmeric
15g butter or vegetable oil
2 tablespoons finely chopped red onion
1 ripe tomato, cut into small pieces
1 to 3 teaspoons thinly sliced chilli
1 tablespoon chopped coriander
Salt and freshly ground black pepper
Ketchup, for serving (optional)

This breakfast was inspired by my Pakistani father, who loves to tuck into a cumin and green chilli omelette on the weekends. As tolerance for heat from chilli varies, I've suggested a range, depending on how much kick you like. Some buttered toast or wholewheat rotis would be a lovely accompaniment, as would ketchup or sriracha and a mug of hot, sweet, milky chai. This recipe serves one but can easily be scaled up. I've suggested a range of eggs depending on how hungry you are!

Crack the eggs into a small bowl and beat them with the milk, cumin, turmeric, and a good pinch each of salt and pepper.

Melt the butter in a small frying pan over medium heat. Add the onion and cook for 3 to 5 minutes, until soft. Stir in the tomato and chilli and season with a bit more salt. Cook for another minute or two, stirring often.

Spread the vegetables evenly around the pan with a spatula. Add the eggs and swirl them around so they coat the bottom of the pan and fill any gaps. Sprinkle the coriander on top and turn the heat down to low. Cook for a few minutes, until the eggs have just set (you can pop your bread in the toaster at this point!), then flip half of the egg over and cook the omelette through. If you like, you can finish the omelette under a hot grill. Serve immediately.

Smoky Tofu Shakshuka

SERVES 4

3 tablespoons vegetable oil
1 small onion, finely chopped
2 garlic cloves, finely grated
1 teaspoon smoked sweet paprika
½ teaspoon ground cumin
Pinch ground nutmeg or allspice
1 (400g) tin chopped tomatoes
2 teaspoons rose, apricot, or regular harissa
1 teaspoon sugar
1 400g block silken tofu
Salt and freshly ground black pepper

This vegan version of the classic North African scramble uses soft silken tofu instead of eggs without any sacrifice of flavour. I like the sweetness that comes from using a rose or apricot harissa, but regular harissa will work well too – as always, use what you can find and what you prefer! As the spice and heat levels of different brands of harissa can vary quite dramatically, start with my suggestion and then you can always add extra as a condiment when serving. The tomato sauce can be made ahead of time and keeps well in the fridge for up to a week.

Heat the oil in a frying pan over medium heat. Add the onion and ½ teaspoon salt and cook for about 12 minutes, until the onion has softened.

Add the garlic, paprika, cumin, and nutmeg and cook for 2 minutes, stirring often. Stir in the tomatoes, harissa, sugar, another ¼ teaspoon salt, and a generous grind of pepper. Bring to the boil, then reduce the heat, cover, and simmer for 20 minutes, stirring occasionally.

Add the tofu, gently breaking it up as you fold it into the tomato mixture. Cook for 2 minutes, then taste and add a touch more salt and pepper or harissa if needed.

Banana and Tahini Pancakes

MAKES 12 PANCAKES

1 large banana
2 tablespoons runny tahini
1 teaspoon vanilla extract
½ teaspoon ground cinnamon
240g plain flour
1½ teaspoons baking powder
360ml unsweetened plant-based milk
Vegetable oil
Fine salt

TOPPINGS

Date syrup
Runny tahini
Fresh berries or more chopped banana

These deliciously fluffy and light pancakes just happen to be vegan. Date syrup and tahini are a classic Levantine breakfast pairing and work well as a topping for the pancakes, though you can of course go with the classic maple syrup drizzle on top. Your breakfast, your rules! The pancakes are best served warm, so either plate them up as you make them or turn the oven on low before you start cooking and leave the pancakes on a baking sheet lined with baking paper to stay warm while you make the full batch. Depending on how large your pan is, you should be able to cook a few at a time.

Mash the banana with a fork in a large bowl until smooth and lump-free. Add the tahini, vanilla, cinnamon, and ¼ teaspoon salt and mix well. Add the flour and baking powder and mix until fully incorporated, then add the milk and lightly beat together until a thick batter forms.

Heat 1 to 2 tablespoons oil in a large frying pan over medium heat and swirl it around so the pan is well coated. Working in batches, add a small ladle (about 3 tablespoons) batter per pancake. As soon as you can see bubbles appear on the surface of the pancakes, usually after 2 to 3 minutes, gently flip them and cook for another few minutes on the other side, until golden brown.

To serve, drizzle with the date syrup and tahini and top with a handful of fresh berries.

Fu'ul Mudamas

SERVES 4 WITH BREAD AND ACCOMPANIMENTS

- 1 tablespoon vegetable oil
- 2 garlic cloves, finely grated
- 2 (400g) tins broad or pinto beans, undrained
- 1½ teaspoons ground cumin
- 1 green chilli, deseeded and chopped, or more to taste
- 2 to 3 tablespoons lemon juice
- 1 ripe tomato, roughly chopped
- 2 tablespoons tahini
- 2 to 3 tablespoons water
- 2 tablespoons chopped parsley
- Extra-virgin olive oil
- Flatbread and Middle Eastern pickled turnip and cucumber, for serving
- Salt and freshly ground black pepper

The appearance and simplicity of this classic North African and Levantine dish belies its splendour. The humble combination of mashed beans with cumin, olive oil, garlic, and lemon juice might not be much to look at on its own, but when combined with the accompaniments, it feels like a real feast – as well as being an incredibly healthy way to start your day. But don't restrict this meal to breakfast or brunch; you can eat it anytime. There are dozens of different versions of this dish throughout the region, and my version is fairly abridged, using tinned beans, which means it can be on the table in 15 minutes from start to finish. You can find cooked broad beans in Middle Eastern supermarkets, but feel free to substitute pinto beans as I often do. I like to add a tahini sauce and hard-boiled eggs for an extra protein hit. Most important are the pickled, sour accompaniments such as kabees, the Levantine bright pink batons of pickled turnips, or Middle Eastern fermented cucumber pickles. Serve alongside bread; Arabic flatbread is most authentic, but I usually eat it with wholewheat pitta as that's what I most commonly have stashed in my freezer.

Heat the vegetable oil in a large saucepan over medium heat. Add 1 finely grated garlic clove and cook for 1 or 2 minutes, stirring frequently, until golden. Add the beans and their liquid, then the cumin. Bring to a boil, reduce the heat, and simmer for 5 minutes.

While the beans are cooking, combine the chopped chilli, remaining finely grated garlic clove, 1 tablespoon of the lemon juice, and a generous pinch of salt in a mortar and pestle. Smash everything together. Transfer to a small bowl, add the tomato, and mix well.

continues ▶

Take the beans off the heat and use a potato masher, wooden spoon, or the back of a fork to roughly mash half of them. Taste and adjust the seasoning if needed – you might want to add a touch more salt. Cook for another 2 minutes to thicken the sauce.

In a small bowl, mix the tahini, water, remaining lemon juice, and a pinch of salt until you have a thick sauce. Pour the beans into a large serving bowl, spoon the tahini sauce over them, and top with the garlicky tomato and a scattering of fresh parsley. Finish with a drizzle of olive oil and serve immediately with flatbreads and pickles.

Big Salads

Let the salad-maker be a spendthrift for oil,
a miser for vinegar, a statesman for salt,
and a madman for tossing.

– **SPANISH PROVERB**

If I'm eating a salad, I want it to be big. Big in flavour, big in texture, big in visual appeal. These are the kinds of salads I've included in this chapter: colourful, crunchy, and crammed with appeal. I grew up in a household where salad was present with every meal, dressed with a peppery slick of extra-virgin olive oil and a sharp vinegar to cut through the hearty Iranian stews my mum cooked. This juxtaposition of hot and cold, soft and structured, rich and acidic brought a refreshing balance to the meals we ate, which is one of the secrets of a meal's success. In that spirit, I'd encourage you to always include a type of salad at your dining table for freshness. It could simply be a plate of fresh herbs with some sliced radishes, or a classic tomato, cucumber, and lettuce salad, or one of the recipes from this chapter. I encourage you to play around with ingredients you might not typically add to a salad, such as fresh or dried fruits, raw root vegetables, and, of course, fresh herbs. Salads can be made from a whole host of raw and cooked vegetables; the only limit is your imagination! And, as the Spanish proverb above stipulates, season well and get your (clean) hands in the bowl to properly toss everything together. You'll be rewarded for it.

Broccoli and Lentil Salad
with Curried Tahini and Dates

SERVES 4 TO 6
AS PART OF A MEZZE

ROASTED VEGETABLES
700g broccoli (about 2 crowns)
140g radishes (about 16 small red round ones)
2 tablespoons vegetable oil
Salt

LENTILS
240g Puy lentils (see headnote)
600ml just-boiled water
2 tablespoons extra-virgin olive oil
3 tablespoons lemon juice
Salt and freshly ground black pepper

CURRIED TAHINI SAUCE
120g tahini
75ml lemon juice
60ml water
1 garlic clove, finely grated
1 tablespoon maple syrup
1 teaspoon medium curry powder
Salt and freshly ground black pepper

TOPPINGS
6 Medjool dates, pitted and roughly chopped
1 small handful chopped parsley or coriander leaves (optional)

Tahini sauces are wonderful vehicles for adding creaminess to dishes without the need for dairy. Here broccoli florets and radishes are first roasted and then dressed with a curry-spiced tahini dressing and served on a bed of lentils. Pair this with something light and sharp, such as the Fennel, Avocado, and Pistachio Salad (page 61) and crusty sourdough bread for a fabulously flavoursome and healthy meal. Giving exact measurements for tahini dressings can be tricky as each brand varies so much in thickness (and on how long you've had the jar open), so use the recipe below as a guide and add a touch more water or lemon to loosen, or extra tahini to thicken. I've suggested Puy lentils for this dish as they hold their shape so well, but they are more expensive. You can use regular brown or green lentils instead – just reduce the cooking time as they normally soften in 15 to 20 minutes, depending on their freshness. (See the photo on page 57.)

Preheat the oven to 200°C/Fan 180°C/Gas Mark 6.

Break up the broccoli florets and slice off the stalks as they naturally separate. Slice the stalks into thick pieces about the same size as the florets. Put the broccoli and radishes on a large baking sheet and toss with the vegetable oil and ½ teaspoon salt. Roast for about 20 minutes, until cooked but still firm. The broccoli will be slightly charred and that's OK! Set aside to cool.

While the vegetables are in the oven, combine the lentils and just-boiled water in a small saucepan, cover, and cook over medium heat for 25 to 30 minutes, until the lentils are soft but still have some shape. Drain and return to the saucepan, then dress with the olive oil, the lemon juice, ½ teaspoon salt, and ¼ teaspoon pepper.

To make the curried tahini sauce, whisk together the tahini, lemon juice, water, garlic, maple syrup, curry powder, ½ teaspoon salt, and ¼ teaspoon black pepper in a small bowl. The sauce will thicken as it sits, so if you are making it ahead of time, you might need to add more water.

To serve, spread the lentils in a shallow serving dish, spoon over two-thirds of the tahini sauce, pile the roasted broccoli and radishes on top, drizzle over the remaining tahini sauce, and scatter the dates and herbs (if using) on top.

Fennel, Avocado, and Pistachio Salad

SERVES 4 TO 6

2 heads Little Gem lettuce (about 230g)
1 fennel bulb, thinly sliced
1 large handful mint leaves, finely chopped
1 large handful parsley leaves, finely chopped
1 small handful tarragon leaves
3 tablespoons pistachios
2 ripe avocados, sliced

DRESSING

3 tablespoons extra-virgin olive oil
2 tablespoons lemon juice
1 tablespoon white wine vinegar or apple cider vinegar
Salt and freshly ground black pepper

This fragrant salad celebrates the delicate flavours of anise with its thin shavings of crunchy fennel and tangles of tarragon, which come together to make a highly aromatic side dish. Tarragon is one of the most underused herbs in Western cooking, but Iranians love it and it's an essential component of Sabzi Khordan (page 110). I adore its peppery, aniseed flavour, and if I'm buying it for this salad, I like to use the rest finely chopped into an omelette or strewn across some feta and cucumber in a sandwich. Using a mandoline will help you slice the fennel finely (I use the thickest settings on mine to make this). Just be careful of your fingers!

Combine the lettuce leaves, fennel, and herbs in a large bowl.

Toast the pistachios in a pan over medium heat for 2 to 3 minutes. Transfer to a chopping board, roughly chop, and add to the salad.

Make the dressing by whisking together the olive oil, lemon juice, vinegar, ½ teaspoon salt, and ¼ teaspoon pepper in a small bowl. Pour over the salad leaves and then use your (clean!) hands to mix it all together, ensuring every leaf is covered with some dressing. Add the avocado and lightly toss again, until coated. Taste and adjust the seasoning – depending on what you are serving this with, you may want a touch more salt or vinegar.

Roast Potato, Asparagus, and Sun-Dried Tomato Salad

SERVES 4

1kg new potatoes
Vegetable oil
200g asparagus tips (about 18 stalks)
2 large handfuls rocket leaves
2 tablespoons finely sliced spring onions
6 sun-dried tomato halves, roughly chopped
1 large handful basil leaves, roughly torn
1 (125g) fresh mozzarella ball (optional)
Aleppo pepper or other mild chilli flakes
Salt

DRESSING

2 tablespoons extra-virgin olive oil
1½ tablespoons lemon juice
½ teaspoon ground allspice
1 garlic clove, smashed with the side of a knife
Salt and freshly ground black pepper

I love making this salad when the first new potatoes of the year arrive and the joy of outdoor eating returns. But any kind of waxy potato will do, just choose what is most easily available to you. Roasting the potatoes gives the salad a wonderful, crispy texture, and sun-dried tomatoes evoke memories of sun-tinged travels through Italy and Turkey. The mozzarella is optional – I love the contrast of the soft pieces strewn across the crunchy asparagus, but it's just as good without.

Preheat the oven to 200°C/Fan 180°C/Gas Mark 6.

On a large baking sheet, toss the potatoes with 2 tablespoons vegetable oil and ¼ teaspoon salt. Roast for about 50 minutes, until tender inside and crispy and golden on the outside. After 40 minutes, toss the asparagus in a little vegetable oil and a sprinkle of salt, and add these to the potatoes for the last 10 minutes of their roasting time.

Meanwhile, make the dressing by whisking together the olive oil, lemon juice, allspice, smashed garlic clove, ¼ teaspoon salt, and ¼ teaspoon pepper in a small bowl. Set aside to infuse for at least 15 minutes.

When the potatoes have cooked, set them aside until cool enough to handle. Use your hands to roughly tear them into halves or, if they are big, into quarters. Transfer them to a large bowl and add the rocket, spring onions, and sun-dried tomatoes. Remove the garlic from the dressing and then pour the dressing over the salad. Mix well. Gently fold in the basil. If you are adding the mozzarella, tear it into chunks and nestle around the potatoes. Finish with a sprinkling of chilli flakes.

Freekeh Pilaf with Cauliflower, Almonds, and Cherries

SERVES 4 TO 6

CAULIFLOWER

1 medium head cauliflower
Olive oil
2 teaspoons ground cumin
½ teaspoon ground allspice
Salt

FREEKEH

200g cracked freekeh
950ml just-boiled water
25g flaked almonds
Extra-virgin olive oil
2 tablespoons lemon juice, or more to taste
50g dried cherries, roughly chopped
1 large handful parsley leaves, roughly chopped
1 teaspoon sumac
Salt and freshly ground black pepper

YOGHURT SAUCE

250g full-fat Greek-style yoghurt or plant-based yoghurt
1 tablespoon lemon juice
½ garlic clove, finely grated
3 tablespoons chopped parsley leaves
Salt

I first learned about freekeh when visiting a women's cooperative near Nablus, in Palestine, through the Canaan food producers' network. They are a remarkable social enterprise that supplies stores in the US and UK and are a great way to directly support Palestinian farmers. If you've never tried the grain before, it's a type of smoky, whole-grain wheat and is great for pilafs (as well as for stuffing vegetables or thickening soups). When buying it, I recommend checking the label to make sure you have the cracked variety, as the whole-grain versions can take much longer to cook. You can replace the dried cherries with cranberries, and for a vegan option simply use a plant-based yoghurt.

Preheat the oven to 200°C/Fan 180°C/Gas Mark 6.

Remove the leaves from the cauliflower and put them on a large baking sheet. Cut the cauliflower into florets about 5cm thick and add those to the baking sheet (you might need two sheets to ensure everything cooks evenly). Toss the leaves and florets with 2 tablespoons olive oil, the cumin, allspice, and ½ teaspoon salt. Roast for 20 minutes, or until the cauliflower has softened and browned.

Meanwhile, rinse the freekeh and put it in a saucepan with the just-boiled water and ¼ teaspoon salt. Cover and cook over medium heat for 20 to 25 minutes, until soft.

While the freekeh and cauliflower are cooking, prepare the yoghurt sauce. In a small bowl, whisk together the yoghurt, lemon juice, garlic, parsley, and ¼ teaspoon salt. Set aside to let the flavours infuse.

Toast the almonds in a small frying pan over medium heat for 1 to 2 minutes, until golden, then remove from the heat.

continues ▶

When the freekeh is cooked, drain and leave in a colander for a few minutes to allow most of the steam to evaporate. Transfer to a large bowl and dress with 2 tablespoons of extra-virgin olive oil, the lemon juice, ¼ teaspoon salt, and a generous grind of black pepper. Add the toasted almonds, chopped cherries, and most of the parsley and toss everything together. Taste and adjust the seasoning.

Gently layer the cauliflower on top of the freekeh. Spoon over the yoghurt sauce (I like to do about 6 large dollops) and finish with a sprinkle of the remaining parsley, a generous smattering of sumac, and a final drizzle of extra-virgin olive oil.

Loaded Wedge Salad
with Tahini Ranch and Crispy Chickpeas

SERVES 4

TAHINI RANCH DRESSING

180g tahini
80ml water
80ml lemon juice
1 tablespoon white wine vinegar or apple cider vinegar
2 teaspoons Dijon mustard
2 teaspoons maple syrup
1 teaspoon garlic granules
1 teaspoon onion granules
3 tablespoons finely chopped chives
3 tablespoons finely chopped parsley
Salt and freshly ground black pepper

CRISPY CHICKPEAS

1 (400g) tin chickpeas, drained and rinsed
1 teaspoon ground cumin
½ teaspoon smoked paprika
2 tablespoons olive oil
Salt and freshly ground black pepper

SALAD

1 iceberg lettuce, cored and quartered or cut into large wedges
1 large ripe avocado, diced
100g soft blue cheese, crumbled

This indulgent salad uses a rich tahini sauce to load up wedges of lettuce before topping them with chunks of avocado, crunchy chickpeas, and crumbled blue cheese. (See the photo on page 68.) Use iceberg wedges or a few halved heads of Little Gem lettuce. Any leftover dressing can be stored in the fridge for up to 3 days (it works great as a dip for crudités or crisps!) – just be aware that tahini thickens, so simply loosen with a little water or lemon juice before serving. Tahini also can vary in terms of how much salt and acidity it needs, so feel free to adjust the salt and vinegar levels accordingly.

To make the dressing, mix the tahini, water, lemon juice, vinegar, mustard, maple syrup, garlic granules, onion granules, chives, parsley, ¾ teaspoon salt, and ¼ teaspoon pepper in a small bowl. Taste and adjust the seasoning. Brands of tahini can vary immensely in flavour and texture, which will result in carrying the ingredients differently – so be confident in adding a dash more maple syrup, salt, or vinegar to balance out the sweet, salty, and acidic notes this dressing needs. Set aside for 1 hour for the flavours to come together.

Preheat the oven to 200°C/Fan 180°C/Gas Mark 6. Line a large baking sheet with foil or baking paper.

On the prepared baking sheet, toss the chickpeas with the cumin, paprika, ¼ teaspoon salt, ¼ teaspoon pepper, and olive oil until well combined. Bake for 20 to 25 minutes, until crisp and golden.

To serve, begin with a layer of dressing on each lettuce wedge, then the avocado, then the crispy chickpeas, and finally the blue cheese. Serve immediately.

Courgette, Pea, and Bulgar Pilaf

SERVES 4

This fragrant salad uses bulgar wheat as its base, an endlessly versatile, slightly chewy grain that is very popular throughout the eastern Mediterranean, where it is used to stuff vegetables, thicken soups, and serve in warm or cold pilafs such as this one. The grains hold their shape and texture well when dressed, making them handy for preparing in advance and great for picnics. To make this dish more substantial I sometimes add a block of feta, crumbled into large chunks.

DRESSING

- 2 tablespoons extra-virgin olive oil
- 3 tablespoons lemon juice
- ½ garlic clove, crushed
- 1½ teaspoons sumac
- ½ teaspoon ground allspice
- Salt and freshly ground black pepper

- 3 medium courgettes (500g), halved diagonally and cut crosswise into large pieces
- Vegetable oil
- 100g bulgar wheat
- 115g frozen peas
- 25g flaked almonds
- Grated zest of 1 lemon
- 2 large handfuls mint leaves, roughly chopped
- 2 large handfuls parsley, roughly chopped
- Salt

Preheat the oven to 200°C/Fan 180°C/Gas Mark 6.

To make the dressing, whisk together the olive oil, lemon juice, garlic, sumac, allspice, ½ teaspoon salt, and ¼ teaspoon pepper in a small bowl. Set aside to allow the acidity of the lemon to mellow out the raw garlic.

On a large baking sheet, toss the courgette pieces with 2 tablespoons vegetable oil and ½ teaspoon salt. Roast for 12 to 15 minutes, until they are soft but still have some bite. Set aside to cool to room temperature.

Meanwhile, put the bulgar in a saucepan and top it with enough just-boiled water to cover the grains by 2.5cm. Cook over medium heat for about 15 minutes, until soft. When the grains are ready, add the frozen peas and cook for another 2 minutes. Drain, rinse under cold running water, and leave in a fine-mesh sieve in the sink for the excess water to drain.

Toast the almonds in a dry frying pan over medium heat for a few minutes until golden brown, then remove from the heat.

Transfer the bulgar and peas to a large bowl. Add the dressing, lemon zest, and herbs and toss well. Fold in half of the almonds and the courgette, taste to adjust the seasoning, then top with the remaining almonds.

Spicy Tomatoes with Walnuts and Pomegranates

SERVES 4 TO 6
AS PART OF A MEZZE

This punchy salad is known as Gavurdağ salatasi in Turkish and gets its name from the Gavur Mountains in the eastern part of the country. As with all tomato salads, the quality of the fruit will determine how tasty the finished dish is, so buy the best available. I like to serve this as part of a spread of mezze-style starters, alongside some flatbreads to mop up its spicy and sour juices. Make sure you buy pomegranate molasses without any added sugar and be sure to use fresh walnuts, as they can very quickly become rancid and bitter. (I store mine in an airtight jar in the fridge to make them last longer.) I recommend making this salad about 30 minutes before you want to serve it to give time for the dressing to infuse the ingredients.

SALAD

680g ripe tomatoes, cut into small pieces
125g walnuts, finely chopped
1 large handful mint leaves, finely chopped
1 large handful parsley leaves, finely chopped
3 spring onions, finely sliced

DRESSING

3 tablespoons extra-virgin olive oil
2 tablespoons lemon juice
2 tablespoons pomegranate molasses
1 small garlic clove, finely grated
1½ teaspoons sumac
1½ teaspoons Aleppo pepper or other mild chilli flakes
Salt and freshly ground black pepper

Combine the tomatoes, walnuts, herbs, and spring onions in a large bowl.

To make the dressing, whisk together the olive oil, lemon juice, pomegranate molasses, garlic, sumac, chilli flakes, ¾ teaspoon salt, and ¼ teaspoon black pepper in a small bowl.

Pour the dressing over the salad and toss well. Set aside for 15 minutes, then taste and adjust the seasoning. This is a dish that is supposed to be sharp and spicy, so you may want to add more lemon, chilli flakes, and salt to your taste.

Castelfranco with Pear and Gorgonzola

SERVES 4 AS A STARTER
OR 2 AS A LIGHT MEAL

1 large, firm head Castelfranco (about 200g)

50g walnuts, roughly chopped

1 pear, cored and thinly sliced

50g soft blue cheese, cut into small cubes

DRESSING

2 tablespoons extra-virgin olive oil

1 tablespoon white wine vinegar or apple cider vinegar

¾ teaspoon Dijon mustard

Salt and freshly ground black pepper

Castelfranco is a peppery heirloom lettuce that is part of the radicchio family but has a milder taste. You can find it at farmers' markets or speciality greengrocers, or substitute regular radicchio or curly-leaf frisée. I most commonly use a soft blue cheese such as Gorgonzola or Roquefort, but a good Stilton also works well. The measurements are approximations; depending on the size of your lettuce or pear you may want to use a little more or less, so you have a balanced mixture of leaves and fruit slices to feed four people.

Place the Castelfranco leaves in a large salad bowl.

Toast the walnuts in a small frying pan over medium heat for a minute or two, until they turn glossy. Remove from the heat and add to the salad bowl.

To make the dressing, whisk together the olive oil, vinegar, mustard, and salt and pepper to taste in a small bowl. Pour over the salad and mix well to ensure each lettuce leaf is fully coated.

Add the pear and blue cheese and toss gently. Taste and adjust the seasoning (you might want more salt or acidity) and serve immediately.

Gazan Tomato Salad

SERVES 4 TO 6
AS PART OF A MEZZE

I was introduced to the many delicacies of Gazan cuisine through Laila El-Haddad's wonderful book *The Gaza Kitchen*, which is a treasure trove of incredible recipes that celebrate the people and culture of Palestinians from Gaza. It's a regional cuisine that is renowned for its unique, punchy combinations of dill, garlic, and green chilli. This salad is a version of a dish I ate at Palestinian restaurant Akub in Notting Hill, where head chef Fadi Kattan has brought a beautiful slice of Palestine to West London. It's a simple dish, which means of course that the produce needs to be at its best for it to shine. Try this salad as part of a mezze; it offers a welcome zesty and bright contrast to richer dishes.

DRESSING

- 1 garlic clove, crushed
- 1 tablespoon finely chopped green chilli, or more to taste
- 3 tablespoons extra-virgin olive oil
- 2 tablespoons lemon juice, or more to taste
- Salt and freshly ground black pepper

- 800g ripe tomatoes, cut into 2cm pieces
- 3 tablespoons finely chopped dill

To make the dressing, whisk together the garlic, chilli, olive oil, lemon juice, ½ teaspoon salt, and ¼ teaspoon pepper in a small bowl. Set aside for 15 minutes so the raw garlic can mellow in the acidity of the lemon juice.

Put the tomatoes in a large bowl and use a potato masher or fork to lightly smash them a few times so they are slightly crushed but still holding together.

Pour the dressing over the tomatoes and stir well. Add the dill, stir again, and taste and adjust the seasoning – you might want to squeeze in more lemon or, if you'd prefer some extra heat, scatter over more green chilli. Serve immediately.

Peach and Feta Salad

SERVES 4 AS A SIDE OR
2 AS A MAIN, WITH BREAD

1 medium Persian cucumber or ¼ regular cucumber (about 170g), cut into small pieces
12 cherry tomatoes (about 170g), halved
1 or 2 ripe peaches (250g), sliced into wedges
1 large handful mint leaves, finely chopped
2 large handfuls parsley leaves, finely chopped
85g crunchy lettuce, such as romaine or Little Gem, roughly sliced
2 tablespoons mixed sesame seeds and pumpkin seeds
100g feta cheese

DRESSING
2 tablespoons extra-virgin olive oil
2 tablespoons lemon juice, or more to taste
2 teaspoons sumac
¼ teaspoon ground allspice
Salt and freshly ground black pepper

This refreshing, summery salad is inspired by the flavours of the Middle East, with a sumac and allspice – spiked dressing. I always use Persian cucumbers for these types of salads as they have a sweeter and more pronounced flavour. If you use a larger cucumber, you might want to slice it in half and scoop out any watery seeds. As sizes of peaches can vary dramatically, go by weight (or by eye) to make sure they are in proportion to the other vegetables. And it goes without saying, the peaches should be ripe, so this salad tastes best when peaches are in season. If you'd like, you can toss in toasted or fried flatbreads and turn it into a type of fattoush salad.

In a large bowl, combine the cucumber, tomatoes, peaches, herbs, lettuce, and seeds.

To make the dressing, whisk together the olive oil, lemon juice, sumac, allspice, ¼ teaspoon salt, and ¼ teaspoon pepper in a small bowl.

Pour the dressing over the salad and mix well. Taste and adjust the seasoning. You might want a bit more lemon or salt. Roughly crumble the feta into large chunks and sprinkle over the salad. Serve immediately.

Orange, Radish, and Olive Salad

SERVES 4

Vibrant and refreshing, this Moroccan-inspired salad is tossed with a cumin and paprika dressing, evoking, in my mind, the heady and aromatic scents of North African souks. This is a salad where the ingredients can vary immensely – from the acidity of the oranges to the saltiness of the olives – so use your judgment and adjust the quantities if necessary. If your black olives are particularly salty, you can also leave them to soak in cold water for 10 minutes and then drain. I like to use blood oranges when they are in season, or a combination of regular and blood oranges for a more vivid visual appeal.

DRESSING

- 2 tablespoons extra-virgin olive oil
- 2 tablespoons lemon juice
- ½ garlic clove, crushed
- ½ teaspoon ground cumin
- ¼ teaspoon sweet paprika
- Salt and freshly ground black pepper

- 5 or 6 blood oranges or 4 large navel oranges
- 2 or 3 radishes, very thinly sliced
- 60g Kalamata olives, pitted and sliced
- Finely chopped coriander leaves, for serving
- Aleppo pepper or other mild chilli flakes, for serving

To make the dressing, whisk together the oil, lemon juice, garlic, cumin, paprika, ¼ teaspoon salt, and pepper in a small bowl and set aside for the flavours to infuse.

Peel the oranges and slice into thin discs. This is best achieved by cutting the top and bottom off each orange, placing it on a chopping board, and using a sharp knife to slice down the sides, removing the rind and pith.

Put the oranges in a large bowl and pour over the dressing. With your hands, very carefully mix in the dressing, then lift out the orange slices and arrange on a serving plate.

Add the radishes and olives to the bowl with the remainder of the dressing and mix well. Strew the radishes and olives over the oranges, pour over any remaining dressing, and finish with a sprinkle of chopped coriander and chilli flakes.

Tempeh and Broccoli Salad
with Spicy Peanut Dressing

SERVES 2 AS A LIGHT MAIN OR 4 AS A SIDE

Many years ago, I spent a year living on a small island in the Gulf of Thailand, where I briefly worked at a wellness resort. This recipe is inspired by a dish that was always on their menu: marinated pieces of tempeh served on a bed of crunchy and colourful vegetables, with a creamy peanut dressing on the side. Tempeh is made by fermenting whole soy beans, and, if you haven't cooked with it before, this is a good place to start. You can find it in most supermarkets and health-food stores. Its distinctive nutty flavour and texture soaks up marinades better than its sister ingredient tofu. You can marinate the tempeh for anywhere from 1 to 24 hours, then just throw the salad together when you are ready to eat. The spicy peanut dressing keeps well in the fridge for up to 3 days.

TEMPEH

- 2 tablespoons light soy sauce or tamari
- 1 tablespoon lime juice
- 1 tablespoon olive oil
- 1 garlic clove, finely grated
- 1 tablespoon finely grated ginger
- 200g tempeh, cut into bite-size rectangles
- Vegetable oil

SALAD

- 1 head broccoli, sliced
- 80g shredded red cabbage
- 1 medium carrot, shredded
- 1 red pepper, deseeded and thinly sliced
- 2 handfuls rocket leaves
- 1 small handful coriander leaves, finely chopped
- 1 tablespoon extra-virgin olive oil
- 1 tablespoon lime juice, plus lime wedges for serving
- Salt

SPICY PEANUT DRESSING

- 5 tablespoons crunchy peanut butter
- 2 to 3 tablespoons water
- 2 tablespoons light soy sauce or tamari
- 2 tablespoons lime juice
- 2 teaspoons maple syrup
- 1 teaspoon apple cider vinegar
- ½ garlic clove, crushed
- 1 teaspoon finely chopped red chilli
- Salt and freshly ground black pepper

continues ►

Combine the soy sauce, lime juice, 1 tablespoon olive oil, garlic, and ginger in a bowl and mix well. Add the tempeh, stirring well to ensure it is evenly coated. Cover and marinate for at least 1 hour at room temperature or as long as overnight in the refrigerator.

To make the peanut dressing, whisk together the peanut butter, water, soy sauce, lime juice, maple syrup, vinegar, garlic, chilli, ½ teaspoon salt, and a generous grind of pepper in a small bowl. Taste to adjust the seasoning, as brands of peanut butter can vary; you may want to add a touch more water, acidity, or salt.

Heat 2 tablespoons vegetable oil in a frying pan over medium heat. Working in batches as necessary, add the tempeh and cook on both sides until it has crisped up around the edges. Transfer to a plate lined with kitchen paper.

Fill a saucepan with just-boiled water and bring to the boil over medium heat. Add the broccoli and blanch for about 3 minutes, or until just cooked through but still crunchy. Drain and rinse under cold running water to stop further cooking, then leave in a colander for a few minutes for the water to drain.

Combine the broccoli, cabbage, carrot, red pepper, rocket, and coriander in a bowl and toss with 1 tablespoon extra-virgin olive oil, the lime juice, and ¼ teaspoon salt. Add half of the dressing to the salad and toss well. Taste and adjust the seasoning.

Transfer the salad to serving plates, divide the tempeh on top, and offer the remaining dressing on the side to dip into as desired, along with lime wedges.

Everyday Middle Eastern Chopped Salad

SERVES 4 AS A SIDE

- 4 ripe tomatoes (about 400g), chopped
- 3 small Persian cucumbers or 1 regular cucumber (about 300g), chopped
- ½ red onion, chopped
- 5 radishes, chopped

OPTIONAL ADDITIONS/ SUBSTITUTIONS

- Add 1 teaspoon dried mint
- Add 1½ teaspoons chopped deseeded green chilli + 2 tablespoons chopped coriander
- Add chopped peppers
- Substitute spring onions for the red onion
- Swap the cucumbers for celery

DRESSING

- 3 tablespoons extra-virgin olive oil
- 3 to 4 tablespoons lemon juice, or more to taste
- Salt and freshly ground black pepper

The classic chopped tomato and cucumber salad is a mainstay of Middle Eastern cuisine, with each country in the region having variations of it. I always put a version of this recipe in my cookbooks as it pairs well with so many meals, and I've included variations with fresh or dried herbs or chillis. Feel free to adapt and make this recipe your own; just remember, you want some crunch and a lot of lemon and salt in the dressing – it is supposed to be sharp! Try to cut all the vegetables to roughly the same small sizes.

Toss the tomatoes, cucumbers, onion, and radishes in a large bowl. (If you are making a variation of the salad, this is also where you would add any of the alternative ingredients.)

Add the oil, lemon juice, ½ teaspoon salt, and ¼ teaspoon pepper and mix well. Taste and adjust the seasoning. It's supposed to be quite sour, so don't hold back on the lemon juice.

Mezzes, Sides, *and* Snacks

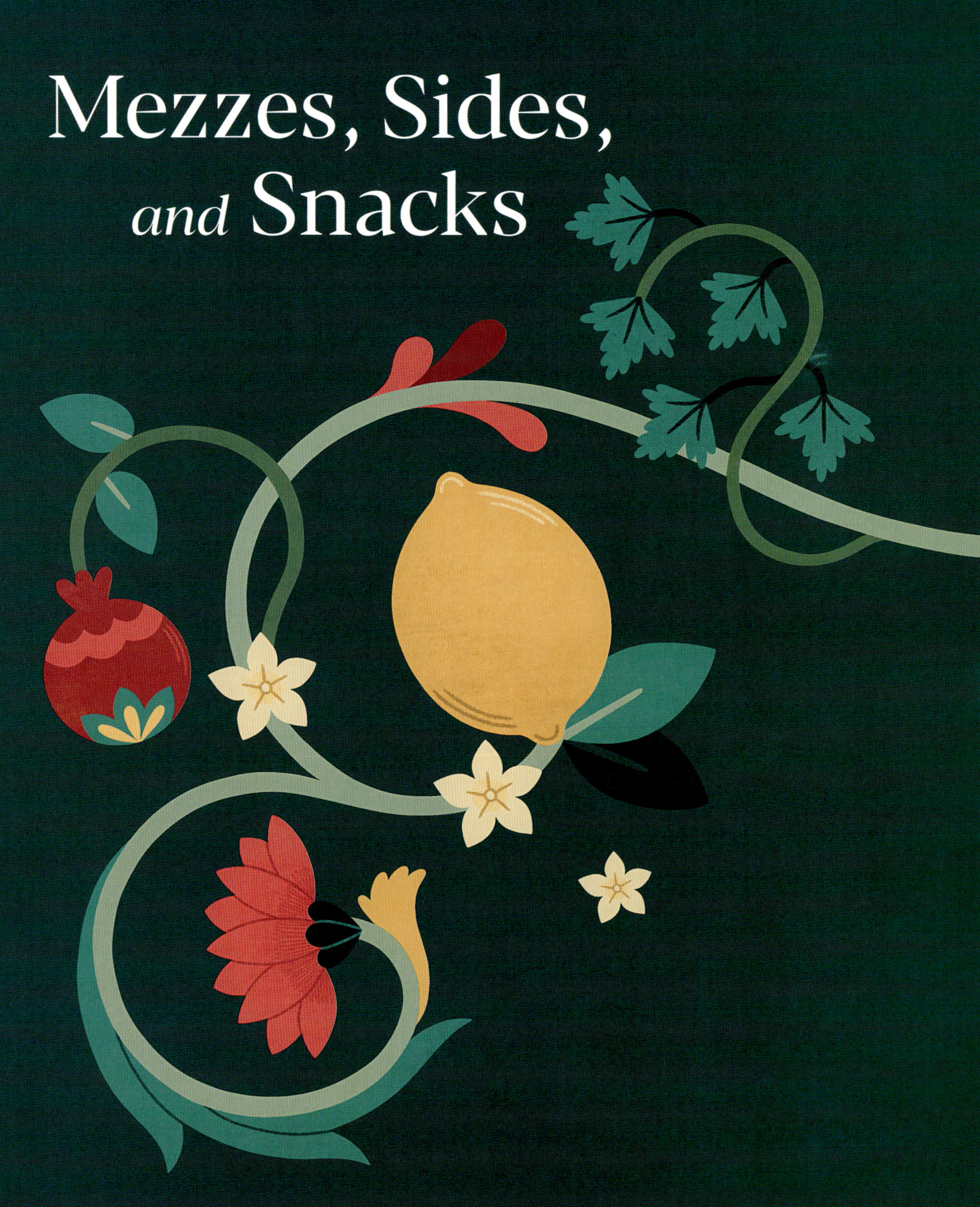

If you really want to make a friend, go to someone's house and eat with him. . . The people who give you their food give you their heart.

– **CÉSAR CHÁVEZ**

For centuries, the people of the Mediterranean and Middle East have been enjoying meals that bring together an assortment of dishes, varying in texture and temperature, for a riotously sensory meal. I've taken inspiration from the flavours of that region for most recipes in this chapter, so you'll find a variety of hot and cold dishes, an abundant use of heady garlic, sticky pomegranate molasses, fragrant herbs, bright lemons, and the subtle sweet heat of Aleppo pepper. Some of these dishes would work well as starters, others as a colourful side dish to a main course, and several, when served together, make for a delightful mezze spread, accompanied by fresh breads to scoop, dip, or wrap around all the beautiful vegetables. There is truly nothing sweeter than leisurely passing around an assortment of plates, each person helping themselves, while sharing good conversation. Don't forget that small bowls of olives and pickles, as well as seasonings such as fresh lemons, chilli flakes, and olive oil, are essential elements to add to your table – they'll deepen the sense of abundance that personifies eating in the mezze style.

Slow-Roasted Carrots
with Tahini Lentils

SERVES 4 TO 6
AS PART OF A MEZZE

Move over, hummus, there's a new spread in town! This cumin and tahini – spiked lentil dip is an excellent alternative to everyone's favourite chickpea snack and is much easier and quicker to make at home. I usually buy a bunch of carrots, still attached to all their leaves, as they tend to be similar in shape and size, which makes the dish when you are layering it up. But if your carrots aren't all the same shape and size, just slice them until they are. This dish keeps well in the fridge for up to 3 days and is best served with bread and a light salad such as Fennel, Avocado, and Pistachio Salad (page 61).

ROAST CARROTS

500g carrots, trimmed
2 tablespoons olive oil
Salt

TAHINI LENTILS

200g brown or green lentils, rinsed
60g tahini
3 tablespoons lemon juice
2 tablespoons water
1 garlic clove, crushed
½ teaspoon ground cumin
Salt

GREEN HERB SMASH

1 handful basil leaves, finely chopped
1 handful parsley leaves, finely chopped
3 tablespoons extra-virgin olive oil
1 teaspoon lemon juice
Salt and freshly ground black pepper

Preheat the oven to 200°C/Fan 180°C/Gas Mark 6.

Toss the whole carrots with 2 tablespoons olive oil and ¼ teaspoon salt on a large baking sheet. Roast for 20 to 25 minutes, until the carrots have softened but still feel firm and are slightly browned. The cooking time will vary depending on the size and age of your carrots, so adjust accordingly.

Meanwhile, put the lentils in a small saucepan and cover with just-boiled water by about 5cm. Bring to the boil, spooning off any scum that rises to the surface. Cook over medium heat for 15 to 20 minutes, until completely soft.

Drain the lentils and transfer to a food processor. Add the tahini, lemon juice, water, garlic, cumin, and ½ teaspoon salt and blend for a minute or two, until smooth. Taste and adjust the seasoning. If it is a little thick, you can add more water. You are aiming for a consistency similar to hummus.

To make the green herb smash, mix the herbs with 3 tablespoons extra-virgin olive oil, the lemon juice, a pinch of salt, and pepper in a mortar and pestle. Smash together until a thick paste forms.

To serve, spoon the lentils into a shallow serving bowl. Top with the carrots, and spoon over the smashed herbs to finish.

Stuffed Aubergine
with Walnuts, Pomegranate, and Feta

SERVES 4 TO 6
AS A MEZZE OR APPETIZER

3 large aubergines
Vegetable oil
2 tablespoons pomegranate molasses
2 tablespoons extra-virgin olive oil
2 tablespoons tahini
½ garlic clove, finely grated
35g walnuts, crushed into fine crumbs
1 handful mint leaves, finely chopped
1 handful coriander leaves, finely chopped
¼ teaspoon golpar
Salt and freshly ground black pepper

TOPPINGS
Crumbled feta cheese
1 handful pomegranate seeds
Finely chopped mint leaves
Sumac

The heady, aromatic flavours of northern Iranian cuisine shine through in this dish, as easy to assemble as it is delicious to eat. The Persian spice golpar is what gives it a unique flavour, adding earthy and citrusy notes that accentuate the pomegranate molasses and lift the notes of fresh mint and coriander. If you can source some online or at an Iranian supermarket, then you are in for a real treat. The aubergine skins can turn chewy after being roasted, so I don't eat them but use them as a vehicle for serving the creamy, garlicky, sweet-and-sour filling. As always, use the freshest walnuts you can find to avoid any bitterness. This dish is served at room temperature, so it can be made a few hours ahead and keeps well in the fridge for up to 2 days.

Preheat the oven to 200°C/Fan 180°C/Gas Mark 6.

Cut the aubergines in half lengthwise. Use a sharp knife to carefully score the inside of each aubergine half on the diagonal, making a crosshatch pattern and being careful not to cut through the skin. Transfer to a large baking sheet, brush with vegetable oil, and sprinkle with salt. Roast for 45 to 60 minutes, until the flesh is soft.

Use a spoon to scoop the aubergine flesh into a bowl. Stir in the pomegranate molasses, olive oil, tahini, garlic, walnuts, mint, coriander, golpar, ¾ teaspoon salt, and a generous grind of black pepper. Taste and adjust the seasoning as needed, then spoon the filling into the aubergine skins and sprinkle over the feta, pomegranate seeds, mint, and sumac.

Butternut Squash and Harissa Dip

SERVES 4 TO 6
AS PART OF A MEZZE

600g peeled and chopped butternut squash
1 tablespoon olive oil
1 (400g) tin white beans, drained and rinsed
2 teaspoons rose harissa, plus more for serving
1 small garlic clove, crushed
1 teaspoon ground cumin
1 teaspoon grated lemon zest
2 tablespoons lemon juice, or more to taste
3 tablespoons extra-virgin olive oil
2 tablespoons pumpkin seeds
Salt and freshly ground black pepper

Many of the meals I prepare at home are a result of opening up the fridge and cupboard and trying to find a way to throw together what I see. This recipe emerged from one of those raids and brings together roasted squash, smashed together with creamy white beans and a few spoons of my favourite rose harissa. The recipe is flexible, so use whatever sweet squash or pumpkin you have, and the same goes for the beans – haricot beans or cannellinis will work. I find this gets the best texture after it's been chilled for at least an hour, so make it ahead of time. It keeps well in the fridge for up to 2 days. Serve with crudités or bread.

Preheat the oven to 180°C/Fan 160°C/Gas Mark 4.

On a large baking sheet, toss the squash with 1 tablespoon olive oil and ½ teaspoon salt. Roast for 25 to 30 minutes, until completely soft.

Transfer the squash to a food processor, add the beans, rose harissa, garlic, cumin, lemon zest and juice, 3 tablespoons extra-virgin olive oil, ½ teaspoon salt, and a generous grind of pepper. Blitz until smooth, then taste and adjust the seasoning. You may want to add a touch more lemon or salt. Transfer to a bowl, cover, and refrigerate for 1 hour.

When ready to serve, toast the pumpkin seeds in a dry pan over medium heat for a minute or two, until they turn glossy. Transfer to a mortar and pestle and smash until broken up slightly. Sprinkle the seeds on top of the dip, along with another drizzle of rose harissa.

Sweet Potatoes
with Pistachio and Mint Pesto

SERVES 4 TO 6
AS PART OF A MEZZE

- 3 large sweet potatoes, scrubbed and cut into thick wedges
- 2 tablespoons extra-virgin olive oil
- A small handful pomegranate seeds
- Salt and freshly ground black pepper

PESTO

- 45g pistachios
- 80ml extra-virgin olive oil
- 1 garlic clove, finely grated
- 1 teaspoon white wine vinegar
- 25g mint leaves
- Salt and freshly ground black pepper

Sweet potatoes are one of my dad's favourite snacks. They remind him of the street food of Punjab, where he grew up. When we were kids, he'd often cook them for us, steaming them in the microwave before slicing them into discs and seasoning with fresh lime juice and salt. It was a sumptuous after-school snack and started my love of sweet potatoes. These days, I prefer to slowly roast them so their sugars begin to caramelise. For this recipe, the roasted wedges are topped with a Sicilian-inspired pesto and finished with a sprinkle of pomegranate seeds. If you have any leftovers, you can serve it with pasta or use as a condiment for cheese or sandwiches.

Preheat the oven to 180°C/Fan 160°C/Gas Mark 4.

On a baking sheet, drizzle the sweet potato wedges with the olive oil and sprinkle with ¼ teaspoon salt and a generous grind of pepper. Use your hands to evenly coat the sweet potatoes. Roast for 40 to 50 minutes, until the sweet potatoes are completely soft. Transfer to a large serving dish to cool.

To make the pesto, toast the pistachios in a small frying pan over medium heat. Lightly stir for 1 to 2 minutes, until they are slightly glossy and release a nutty aroma. Transfer to a food processor and add the olive oil, garlic, vinegar, ¼ teaspoon salt, and ¼ teaspoon pepper. Blend until the nuts are coarsely ground. Add the mint and lightly pulse until a thick pesto forms.

To serve, spoon a few dollops of pesto over each wedge of sweet potato and top with the pomegranate seeds.

White Beans and Mixed Herb Smash

SERVES 2 TO 3 AS A MAIN WITH ACCOMPANIMENTS OR 4 AS PART OF A MEZZE

- 2 tablespoons vegetable oil
- 2 garlic cloves, finely grated
- 2 (400g) tins white beans, drained and rinsed
- 180ml just-boiled water
- Grated zest of 1 lemon
- ¼ teaspoon ground white pepper
- Extra-virgin olive oil
- Salt

MIXED HERB SMASH

- 50g walnuts
- 30g mixed herbs (such as coriander, basil, and parsley), roughly chopped
- 3 tablespoons extra-virgin olive oil
- 1 tablespoon lemon juice
- 1 tablespoon capers, rinsed and roughly chopped
- Salt

These creamy garlic- and lemon-infused beans topped with a herb and nut smash can be prepared in 15 minutes, making this dish perfect for midweek cooking. I use beans in jars for most cooking these days, as I find them to be better seasoned, plumper, and creamier, plus I can easily source them from my local Turkish greengrocer. That said, tinned beans work just as well here, or you could certainly cook the beans from scratch. I make this with cannellini beans, but any kind of white bean will do. I like to serve this with a hunk of sourdough, some boiled new potatoes, and a simple green salad. You'll probably have some leftover herb smash, which you can add to salads, sandwiches, or soups.

Heat the vegetable oil in a large sauté pan over low heat. Add the garlic and cook for 1 minute, stirring frequently so that the garlic doesn't burn. Add the beans, just-boiled water, lemon zest, ¼ teaspoon salt, and white pepper. Using the back of a spoon, crush one-quarter of the beans so you create a thick sauce. Add 1 tablespoon olive oil, cover, turn the heat up to medium, and cook for 5 minutes, until the sauce thickens.

While the beans are cooking, make the herb smash. Put the walnuts in a mortar and pestle and pound until they resemble large breadcrumbs. Add the chopped herbs, 3 tablespoons olive oil, lemon juice, and ¼ teaspoon salt and smash well to form a chunky sauce. Spoon in the chopped capers.

When you are ready to serve, spoon the dressing over each serving of beans and finish with another drizzle of olive oil.

Slow-Cooked Runner Beans

SERVES 6 AS A SIDE, 4 AS A MAIN WITH ACCOMPANIMENTS

- 3 tablespoons olive oil
- 2 medium onions, finely chopped
- 5 garlic cloves, thinly sliced
- 1 (400g) tin chopped tomatoes
- 1½ teaspoons ground cumin
- 1 teaspoon sugar
- ¾ teaspoon smoked paprika
- ½ teaspoon ground cinnamon
- ¼ teaspoon ground allspice
- 600g runner beans, sliced diagonally into 5cm pieces
- 3 tablespoons extra-virgin olive oil
- Salt and freshly ground black pepper

This Turkish-inspired recipe demands cooking the beans long and slow until they are so soft they practically melt in your mouth. The trick to imparting maximum flavour is to properly brown the onions, so don't rush this step. You'll be rewarded with a sweet, lightly spiced, and slightly smoky braised vegetable dish that makes the most of seasonal runner beans. You can serve this as a mezze dish, a vegetable side, or a main course, which is how I most commonly enjoy it, spooned alongside some nutty brown rice, with a good dollop of Greek-style yoghurt on the side. This is best eaten at room temperature, and the flavours improve overnight, so if you can make it ahead and save it until the next day I recommend it.

Heat 3 tablespoons olive oil in a saucepan over medium heat. Add the onions and cook for 20 minutes, until softened and translucent. Add the garlic and cook for 2 minutes. Add the tomatoes, 1½ teaspoons salt, a generous grind of pepper, the cumin, sugar, smoked paprika, cinnamon, and allspice and stir well. Fill the tomato tin with water and swirl it around to get the remaining tomato juice, then add that too. Cover and simmer for 10 minutes, stirring occasionally.

Add the beans and stir well, making sure they are well coated in the tomato sauce. Cover and cook for 35 minutes, or until the beans are completely soft, giving the pot a stir every so often. If the beans start to get dry, you can add more water. When the beans are soft, stir in 3 tablespoons extra-virgin olive oil and cook for a final 2 minutes.

Taste and adjust the seasoning; I like to be generous with the black pepper. You can eat this warm, but I think it's best after it has been left to cool to room temperature, and it tastes even better the next day.

Beetroots
with Whipped Feta and Za'atar

SERVES 4 AS A SIDE OR MEZZE

WHIPPED FETA

150g feta cheese
80g full-fat Greek-style yoghurt
½ garlic clove, finely grated

BEETROOTS

550g cooked beetroots, peeled and cut into 2cm pieces
1 tablespoon lemon juice
Extra-virgin olive oil
1 tablespoon za'atar
2 tablespoons parsley, roughly chopped
1 tablespoon sunflower seeds
Salt and freshly ground black pepper

Sweet beetroots and salty feta are a winning Mediterranean combination. Here they are combined with za'atar, the tangy Levantine spice made from wild thyme, sesame seeds, and sumac, for a vibrant side salad. You can use ready-cooked, vacuum-packed beetroots to save time, but if you want to cook them yourself, I recommend roasting. Simply wrap each beetroot in foil and roast at 200°C/Fan 180°C/Gas Mark 6 for about 1 hour. The skins should peel off easily after they are cooked. Pro tip: If you make this ahead of time, the beetroot juices will seep into the whipped feta, making beautiful pink swirls.

Crumble the feta into a food processor, then add the yoghurt and garlic. Blitz until light and fluffy. Spread on a large plate and smooth it out into a thin layer with the back of a spoon.

In a large bowl, toss the beetroots with the lemon juice, 1 tablespoon oil, za'atar, ¼ teaspoon salt, and ¼ teaspoon pepper (check to see if your za'atar spice mix has salt in it – you may want to use more or less salt accordingly).

Spoon the beetroots on top of the feta and scatter over the chopped parsley. Toast the sunflower seeds in a dry frying pan over medium heat for 1 or 2 minutes, until glossy, then scatter over the beetroots. Finish with another drizzle of oil.

Roast Brussels Sprouts
with Almonds, Coriander, and Pomegranate

SERVES 4 AS A SIDE

700g Brussels sprouts
Olive oil
2 garlic cloves, finely grated
Grated zest of 1 lemon
1 tablespoon lemon juice
1 teaspoon Aleppo pepper or other mild chilli flakes
20g flaked almonds
1 large handful coriander leaves, finely chopped
1 handful pomegranate seeds
Salt and freshly ground black pepper

Growing up in the UK, I always thought I didn't like Brussels sprouts as they were usually served limp and sad, boiled until they were mushy. Spending more time in the US has completely changed my relationship with these versatile cruciferous vegetables and now I absolutely adore them, especially when roasted and slightly charred. This seasonal recipe brings colourful cheer to autumnal and winter tables and would make a lovely side for Christmas.

Preheat the oven to 200°C/Fan 180°C/Gas Mark 6.

On a large baking sheet, toss the Brussels sprouts with 2 tablespoons oil and ¼ teaspoon salt and roast for 25 minutes, until slightly charred.

Meanwhile, heat 2 tablespoons oil in a small frying pan over a low heat. Add the garlic and cook for 1 minute, stirring frequently to ensure it doesn't burn. Transfer the garlic to a large bowl, add the lemon zest and juice, chilli flakes, ¼ teaspoon salt, and ¼ teaspoon black pepper, and mix well.

Put the almonds in the same pan and toast over low heat for 1 or 2 minutes, until lightly golden and fragrant.

When the sprouts are ready, toss them well with the lemon-garlic dressing and add the toasted almonds. Fold in the coriander. Taste and adjust the seasoning, then finish with a handful of pomegranate seeds.

Sekanjabeen

MAKES 350ML

On hot summer days, my mum would make this sweet-and-sour mint concoction for us and place it in a small bowl in the middle of a large platter surrounded by fridge-cold boats of romaine lettuce leaves. We would dunk the lettuce in the dressing and sweep it into our mouths, trying not to make a mess on our clothes along the way. In terms of healthy summer snacks, it doesn't get much better than this. Our Khan family version is an adaptation of the traditional Iranian syrup of simmered mint leaves and vinegar, made using jarred mint sauce, which was what my mum discovered could closely approximate the taste and was easy to source in supermarkets in the 1980s. This is the version I most commonly make, as it's ready in a few minutes, but if you want to make the more traditional syrup, I've included that recipe as well. Sekanjabeen keeps in the fridge for up to 2 days. When serving it, be sure your lettuce leaves are crisp and fridge-cold too.

Speedy version

- 350ml cold water
- 2½ tablespoons mint sauce
- 1 teaspoon apple cider vinegar or white wine vinegar
- 2½ teaspoons granulated sugar
- 1 head romaine lettuce, leaves separated, well chilled
- Salt

In a small bowl, combine the water, mint sauce, vinegar, sugar, and a pinch of salt and stir until the sugar has dissolved. Chill in the fridge, then serve with the lettuce leaves.

Traditional version

- 480ml water
- 100g granulated sugar
- 120ml white wine vinegar
- 2 large handfuls mint leaves
- 1 head romaine lettuce, leaves separated, well chilled

Combine the water, sugar, and vinegar in a small saucepan over medium heat. Bring to the boil, stirring until the sugar dissolves. Add the mint leaves, turn down the heat, and simmer for 25 minutes, until the sauce has reduced. Strain out the mint leaves and leave the syrup to cool. Serve with the lettuce leaves.

Zaalouk (Smoky Aubergine and Tomato Dip)

SERVES 6 AS PART OF A MEZZE

- 3 large aubergines (around 1kg)
- 2 tablespoons vegetable oil
- 4 fat garlic cloves, chopped
- 450g very ripe tomatoes, peeled and grated
- 1 tablespoon tomato purée
- 1 teaspoon smoked sweet paprika
- 1 teaspoon ground cumin
- ½ teaspoon Aleppo pepper or other mild chilli flakes, or more to taste
- 1 large handful parsley, finely chopped
- 1 large handful coriander, finely chopped
- 3 tablespoons extra-virgin olive oil
- Salt and freshly ground black pepper

Throughout North Africa and the Middle East there are an indeterminate number of charred aubergine mezze dishes, each with its own winning combination of mashed aubergine, garlic, and smoke. Zaalouk is a dish I first ate in Morocco and relished its combination of smashed aubergine cooked with sweet tomatoes, cumin, and garlic. You can make this indoors under the grill or outdoors on a barbecue, which imparts a smokier flavour. To peel the tomatoes, use a paring knife to slice a cross at their core and base, then drop them into a pot of just-boiled water for a minute or two. Scoop them out and you should find that the skins easily peel off. The flavours of zaalouk improve over time, so it's a great dish to make ahead. **(See the photo on page 109.)**

If you are cooking indoors, preheat the grill to high. Line a large baking sheet with foil. (If you are cooking outdoors, preheat the barbecue to high.)

Put the aubergines on the prepared baking sheet and use a fork or knife to pierce them several times all over. Roast until the aubergines are charred all over and have collapsed slightly, about 1 hour, turning every 10 to 15 minutes. (If you are cooking outdoors, the process is much quicker, only 15 to 20 minutes.) Once done, run a sharp knife along each aubergine so it splits in half and cools faster.

While the aubergines are cooking, heat the vegetable oil in a pan over medium heat. Add the garlic and cook for about 2 minutes, stirring frequently to ensure it doesn't burn. Add the tomatoes, tomato purée, paprika, cumin, and chilli flakes and cook, stirring often, for 10 minutes.

continues ▶

Once the aubergines are cool enough to handle, scoop out their flesh with a spoon and add it to the pan, along with 1¼ teaspoons salt and a generous grind of black pepper. Turn the heat up to medium-high and cook for 7 minutes, stirring often and using the back of your spoon to mash the aubergine into the tomatoes. You want to evaporate as much water as you can so that the dip thickens.

Add the herbs and olive oil and cook for a final 5 minutes, or until you've achieved a thick consistency (reduce the heat as you see fit). Remove from the heat and set aside for 1 hour, then taste and adjust the seasoning. This works well at room temperature, but you can also rewarm it before serving.

Sabzi Khordan (Iranian Herb Platter)

SERVES 4

1 handful coriander
1 handful tarragon
1 handful mint
1 handful parsley
1 handful basil
1 handful chives
1 handful radishes (with their peppery leaves, if possible)
A few spring onions, sliced into long batons
1 small block feta cheese
1 small handful walnuts

The word *mezze* originates in the Persian word *mazze*, which means "to taste". This platter of fresh herbs, with feta and bread, is commonly served at the start of a meal to do just that: bring your taste buds to life with freshness and brightness. This recipe is incredibly flexible, so take the amounts as suggestions rather than fixed quantities. The stems of coriander, basil, and parsley are edible and full of flavour, so you can include them too. For the mint and tarragon, it's fine to include the stems on the platter unless they are especially thick and chewy, in which case they are best discarded. Try to have at least four different herbs on your plate. Serve alongside flatbreads, or without the cheese and nuts as an accompaniment to Iranian stews such as Aubergine Fesenjan (page 171) or Persian Aubergine, Split Pea, and Dried Lime Stew (Gheimeh Badinjan, page 148). (See a photo of Sabzi Khordan on page 173).

Wash and dry the herbs and trim or pull off any leaves that look past their best. Arrange the herbs on a serving plate. Add the radishes and spring onions and nestle them into the side of the plate. If you are serving with a stew, you can take this to the table as it is, but if you are serving it as a mezze, add a small block of feta and some walnuts.

Punjabi Spiced Vegetable Medley

SERVES 4 TO 6 AS A SIDE

3 tablespoons vegetable oil
1 onion, finely chopped
3 fat garlic cloves, finely grated
1½ tablespoons finely chopped ginger
2 teaspoons cumin seeds
2 teaspoons garam masala
1 teaspoon ground turmeric
1 teaspoon yellow or brown mustard seeds
2 medium potatoes (450g), peeled and cut into small chunks
3 large carrots (250g), peeled and cut into small chunks
250ml water
½ medium cauliflower, broken into florets
130g frozen peas
Coriander leaves, for garnish
Salt

This is my version of a classic Punjabi dish of mixed potatoes, carrots, and peas that my dad often cooks. I like to add cauliflower and make big batches as it keeps well in the fridge and pairs with so many dishes as a side. Try to chop the vegetables into roughly the same-size pieces (the cauliflower is likely to be a bit bigger than the others, but that's OK). The texture of the vegetables you are aiming for is soft but still holding their shape. This isn't the place for crunchy carrots! This goes especially well with the daal recipes in this book (pages 159, 175, and 190) for a delicious South Asian feast. **(See the photo on page 189).**

Heat the oil in a large saucepan over medium-low heat. Add the onion and 1 teaspoon salt and cook for 15 minutes, stirring frequently, until soft.

Add the garlic, ginger, cumin seeds, garam masala, and turmeric, stir well, and cook for 2 minutes. Add the mustard seeds and cook until they start to pop. Add the potatoes, carrots, and 125ml of the water, stir well, cover, and cook for about 12 minutes, until soft, stirring every so often.

Add the cauliflower and remaining 125ml water and stir well. Cover and cook for 8 minutes, until the cauliflower is soft but not falling apart.

Stir in the peas and cook for 3 to 4 minutes, until heated through, adding more water if it looks dry. Taste and adjust the seasoning to your taste, then garnish with coriander to serve.

Aubergine and Barberry Kuku

SERVES 4

- 3 medium aubergines, peeled and cut into 3cm pieces
- Vegetable oil
- Pinch saffron strands
- Pinch sugar
- 1 tablespoon just-boiled water
- 1 medium onion, chopped
- 1 fat garlic clove, crushed
- 6 large eggs
- ½ teaspoon ground turmeric
- ½ teaspoon ground cumin
- 1 tablespoon plain flour
- 1 teaspoon lemon juice
- 2 tablespoons barberries
- 1 large handful finely chopped coriander leaves
- Salt

One of the bedrocks of Iranian cuisine, *kuku* is the Persian word for a dense filled frittata that is often served as a sandwich filling, layered between bread with some slices of tomato and crunchy, salty pickles. This recipe uses aubergine but can easily be subbed with courgette and is packed with the classic Iranian ingredients of saffron, turmeric, and barberries – small, sharp, dried berries that add a wonderful tang to the finished dish. You can source them online, in larger supermarkets, or at Middle Eastern supermarkets. Kukus can be eaten alongside a salad, served as part of a picnic or mezze, or stuffed into pockets of pitta for a snack.

Preheat the oven to 200°C/Fan 180°C/Gas Mark 6.

Spread the aubergines on a large baking sheet. Drizzle with 3 tablespoons oil, sprinkle with 1 teaspoon salt, and toss to coat well. Roast for 20 to 25 minutes, or until completely soft. Set aside to cool.

Meanwhile, grind the saffron and sugar in a mortar and pestle. Add the just-boiled water and let steep for 5 minutes.

Heat 2 tablespoons oil in a medium oven-safe pan over medium heat. Add the onion and cook for 15 minutes, or until soft and brown. Add the garlic and cook for 2 minutes. Tip into a bowl and leave to cool.

In a large bowl, whisk together the eggs, saffron mixture, turmeric, cumin, flour, lemon juice, and ½ teaspoon salt. Fold in the barberries, coriander, aubergine, and onion.

Heat 2 tablespoons oil in the same pan over medium heat. Pour the kuku mixture into the pan, cover, and cook for 8 to 10 minutes, until just cooked through. You want it mostly set and puffing up a bit at the sides.

Turn on the grill. When the kuku is ready, finish it off under the grill until it is set and has turned golden brown on top. Let cool to room temperature before slicing it into thick triangles to serve.

Labneh
with Persimmon and Harissa

SERVES 4

375g labneh or thick, strained Greek-style yoghurt, mixed with a pinch of salt
100g diced persimmon
½ teaspoon harissa (regular, rose, or apricot flavoured)
Squeeze of lemon juice
Aleppo pepper or other mild chilli flakes
Extra-virgin olive oil
A few mint leaves, roughly chopped
Salt

This sweet and spicy dip was inspired by a dish I ate at New York restaurant Shuka several years ago. Perfect for autumn (without a pumpkin in sight!), it works well as an starter or as part of a mezze. I use medium-firm Fuyu persimmons, sometimes called kaki, as they don't have those pesky tannins that can make your mouth feel furry and dry. You can also make this with ripe Hachiya persimmons, but you'll get a squishier, preserve-type filling – although it will still be delicious! If you don't have any harissa, add more chilli flakes. Serve with warm flatbreads.

Spread the labneh with the back of a spoon on a small serving plate.

In a small bowl, mix together the persimmon, harissa, lemon juice, and a pinch of salt, then spoon the mixture into the middle of the labneh. Sprinkle over some chilli flakes, a drizzle of olive oil, and the mint. Serve immediately.

Lentil Kofte

MAKES 16 KOFTE

- 170g red lentils
- 710ml just-boiled water
- 1½ teaspoons ground cumin
- 2 tablespoons vegetable oil
- 1 medium onion, finely chopped
- 4 fat garlic cloves, finely grated
- 100g fine bulgar wheat
- 3 tablespoons tomato purée
- 3 tablespoons extra-virgin olive oil
- 1 tablespoon pomegranate molasses
- 1 large handful parsley leaves, finely chopped
- 1 small handful mint leaves, finely chopped
- 1½ teaspoons grated lemon zest
- 3 tablespoons lemon juice, or more to taste
- 1 teaspoon Aleppo pepper or other mild chilli flakes
- ½ teaspoon smoked paprika
- Salt and freshly ground black pepper

Turkish cuisine is well known for its infinite varieties of meat kofte, but it also has some excellent plant-based ones, such as these small patties of red lentils and fresh herbs known as mercimek köftesi. I shape them into small oval rounds (similar to Middle Eastern kibbeh), but you could also use it as a pâté and spread on toasted bread. These keep well in the fridge for up to 3 days.

Rinse the lentils in cold water. Put them in a saucepan, cover with the just-boiled water, and bring to the boil, using a spoon to remove any scum that rises to the surface. Add the cumin, cover, turn the heat down to medium, and cook for about 15 minutes, or until completely soft.

While the lentils are cooking, heat the vegetable oil in a small pan over medium heat. Add the onion and cook for 15 minutes. Add the garlic and cook for another 2 minutes.

When the lentils are done, stir in the bulgar, cover, turn the heat down to low, and cook for 5 minutes. Add the onion-garlic mixture, along with the tomato purée, olive oil, pomegranate molasses, parsley, mint, lemon zest and juice, chilli flakes, smoked paprika, 1 teaspoon salt, and ¼ teaspoon black pepper. Stir well, then taste and adjust the seasoning.

Leave the mixture to cool for 15 minutes. This is important to enable you to shape the kofte. Lightly grease your palms with a little oil, mould the mixture into small rugby ball shapes, and serve.

Grilled Corn on the Cob
with Feta, Coriander, and Chilli

SERVES 4

- 4 corn cobs, any husks removed
- 125g feta cheese
- 2 tablespoons finely chopped coriander leaves
- Grated zest of ½ lime
- 1½ tablespoons lime juice
- ¼ teaspoon Aleppo pepper or other mild chilli flakes, plus more to serve
- Extra-virgin olive oil
- Salt and freshly ground black pepper

Barbecued corn on the cob is a common street food snack across Iran, and I have countless memories of early evening walks around the bustling markets of Rasht in the northern province of Gilan, stopping off for bites of grilled corn cobs dunked in salt water – they were sweet, smoky, salty, and crunchy all at once! This recipe flips that technique by first boiling the corn in seasoned water and then transferring them to the barbecue. I find it keeps the corn juicier this way, while still imparting a wonderful smoky flavour. You can serve them as they are (in season, sweetcorn needs very little to taste good), but if you want to add some more fun elements, this smashed feta, lime, and coriander topping is a winner.

Bring a large pot of water to the boil and add 1 tablespoon salt. Add the corn on the cobs to the boiling water and cook over medium heat for about 10 minutes, until softened, then drain and set aside for the steam to evaporate.

While the corn is cooking, preheat a barbecue or a griddle pan on the hob.

Mash the feta, coriander, lime zest and juice, chilli flakes, and a generous grind of black pepper together in a small bowl.

When the corn is ready, brush olive oil over each corn cob, then pop them on the hot barbecue or griddle pan, turning every few minutes, until they have blackened on each side.

Transfer the corn to a plate and top with the cheese and herb topping, finishing with a sprinkle of chilli flakes and/or black pepper.

Dalaar

MAKES ABOUT 1 CUP/200G

100g coriander leaves
50g parsley leaves
50g mint leaves
1 tablespoon basil leaves
2 tablespoons salt

Dalaar is a herbed salt from the Caspian Sea region of Iran, where local herbs are finely chopped and pounded to create a pungent and aromatic salty condiment used to spread on cucumbers and acidic fruits such as kiwis, oranges, and sour plums. Traditionally made as a way of preserving fresh herbs in the summer months, dalaar can also be used to flavour yoghurt dishes or drinks and as a marinade for olives and fish. Back in Gilan, it is made with herbs that are almost impossible to source in the West, such as chochagh and khalvash, so my recipe is by no means authentic but still enables me to recreate some of the fresh, salty, herby goodness that I so fondly associate with it. This herbed salt is used very sparingly, so you need only a small amount. Dalaar keeps well in the fridge for up to 2 weeks or in the freezer for up to 3 months.

Wash the herbs and then dry them in a salad spinner or leave them on a tea towel until all their water has evaporated. Transfer to a food processor and blitz with the salt. Store in a small jar in the fridge or freezer.

Yoghurt Boranis

Throughout the Middle East and eastern Mediterranean, yoghurt-based dishes are a central component of mezze, starters, and sides, their cooling properties a welcome balm from the region's heat and sun. Sitting somewhere between what in the West we would identify as a dip and a salad are countless varieties of these dishes incorporating beetroots and dill, cucumbers and mint, or aubergines and garlic (and you can find those recipes in my previous books!). Here are a few more you should get to know.

Spinach Borani

SERVES 4

300g frozen spinach
2 tablespoons water
500g yoghurt
½ small garlic clove, finely grated
1 tablespoon vegetable oil
50g raisins
Extra-virgin olive oil, for serving
Salt and freshly ground black pepper

This is one of our family's favourites, and we always serve it alongside kebabs and rice at barbecues, as well as with Iranian rice dishes such as Aubergine and Lentil Tahchin (page 184). Also great as a dip on its own, it's utterly addictive with crisps or crudités. I use frozen spinach, which is not only more affordable but I feel it also gives the dish a deeper flavour. The borani keeps well in the fridge for up to 2 days.

Put the frozen spinach and water in a small saucepan and cook over medium heat until defrosted. Set aside to cool.

In a bowl, combine the yoghurt, garlic, ½ teaspoon salt, and a generous grind of pepper. Stir in the cooled spinach.

Heat the vegetable oil in a small pan over medium heat and cook the raisins for 1 to 2 minutes, or until starting to plump up. Scatter the raisins over the spinach mixture and finish with a drizzle of olive oil before serving.

Carrot Heydari

SERVES 4

- 2 tablespoons vegetable oil
- 3 garlic cloves, crushed
- 4 medium carrots, grated (250g)
- ½ teaspoon ground cumin
- 500g yoghurt
- 1 tablespoon lemon juice, or more to taste
- 2 tablespoons chopped parsley
- Extra-virgin olive oil, for serving
- Salt and freshly ground black pepper

This dish transports me back to southern Turkey, where I first ate it on a boat trip off the coast of the picturesque town of Kaş. Cooked carrots and yoghurt aren't an obvious pairing, but the thick, cool, garlic-infused yoghurt perfectly complements the sweetness of the carrots. This tastes best after it's had an hour or so to chill and keeps well in the fridge for up to 2 days.

Heat the vegetable oil in a large saucepan over medium heat. Add the garlic and cook for 2 minutes, stirring often. Add the carrots, cumin, and ½ teaspoon salt and cook, stirring often, for 10 minutes, or until the carrots are soft. Set aside to cool.

In a bowl, mix the cooled carrots with the yoghurt, lemon juice, parsley, and a generous grind of pepper. Taste and adjust the seasoning – you may want to add a bit more salt or lemon. Cover and refrigerate for at least 1 hour before serving. When you are ready to eat, drizzle with a bit of olive oil and give it another grind of black pepper before you bring it to the table.

Courgette Borani

SERVES 4

600g courgettes (4 to 5)
Olive oil
250g Greek-style yoghurt
½ small garlic clove, finely grated
1½ teaspoons dried mint
1 teaspoon lemon juice, or more to taste
¼ teaspoon ground white pepper
Aleppo pepper or other mild chilli flakes
Salt

Roast courgettes and dried mint are combined with garlic and yoghurt for this refreshing side, which sings of summer. Dried mint has a uniquely refreshing and cooling impact and is worth seeking out from speciality stores or online if you can't find it in your local supermarket. It has a completely different flavour profile from fresh mint and is used throughout the Eastern Mediterranean to imbue dishes with a menthol-like aroma.

Preheat the oven to 175°C/Fan 160°C/Gas Mark 4.

Roughly cut the courgettes into small chunks. Place on a large baking sheet and toss with 1 tablespoon olive oil and ½ teaspoon salt. Roast for 20 minutes, until completely cooked through and browned all over. Set aside to cool.

Transfer the cooled courgette to a large bowl and mash into a thick paste with a potato masher or the back of a fork. Add the yoghurt, garlic, dried mint, lemon juice, 1 tablespoon olive oil, ¼ teaspoon salt, and white pepper. Cover and refrigerate for 1 hour, then taste and adjust the seasoning – you may want a touch more salt or lemon juice. Sprinkle over a little pinch of chilli flakes just before you bring it to the table.

Soups for Every Season

Real soup is to the body what peace is to the soul.
– **ISABEL ALLENDE**

Soup is my treasured and beloved companion that I turn to when life feels just a little bit harder than I'd like it. I can eat it for breakfast, lunch, dinner, and those in-between times, too, when I need a snack. It is also probably one of the first dishes I seek out in new countries. I have vivid memories of sipping spoonfuls of warm, garlicky almond soup at the foot of Mount Etna in Sicily, tucking into creamy bowls of mushroom and pearl barley soup on a snowy day in Tehran, and warding off the threat of a cold with a fiery hot and sour tom yam in Bangkok. My love of soup means I always have several different types in the freezer, carefully divided into individual portions, which I defrost in the microwave or on the hob for a meal in minutes. The soups in this chapter range from smooth, chilled, and refreshing to chunky, robust, and filling. People who complain that soups are boring because each spoonful is the same completely miss the point. It's the repetitive nature of each mouthful that is inherent to its calming properties. Life is hectic and busy enough; soup doesn't have to be.

Smoky Black Bean Soup

SERVES 4

250g black beans
1 medium onion, roughly chopped
4 fat garlic cloves, finely grated
2 bay leaves
2 teaspoons cumin seeds
1½ teaspoons smoked sweet paprika
1 teaspoon dried oregano
½ teaspoon Aleppo pepper or other mild chilli flakes
¼ teaspoon ground allspice
1 tablespoon tomato purée
500ml vegetable stock
60ml extra-virgin olive oil
500ml just-boiled water
Salt and freshly ground black pepper

TOPPINGS (MIX AND MATCH AS YOU PREFER)

Soured cream or yoghurt
Sliced avocado
Lime wedges
Thinly sliced radishes
Chopped coriander leaves
Sliced jalapeño or additional chilli flakes

I spent large stints of my twenties travelling around Latin America, each time returning with innumerable ingredients and foodie artifacts from those trips. These included an arepa maker from Venezeula, a mojito muddler from Cuba, and a large molcajete granite mortar and pestle from Mexico. I also brought back a love of black beans, which are eaten throughout the continent in various guises. This soup is inspired by those dishes and can be eaten as a soup as pictured or, by skipping the suggestion to add water toward the end, not mashing the beans, and reducing the liquid, can be spooned over rice, stuffed into tacos, or served over nachos. This is one recipe that really benefits from cooking dry beans from scratch, but if you don't have the time, two (400g) tins, drained and rinsed, can be substituted. (See the photo on page 129.)

Put the beans in a large bowl, cover with water, and stir in 2 teaspoons salt. Leave to soak for 8 hours or overnight. Drain and rinse.

Transfer the beans to a large saucepan and top with just-boiled water, covering the beans by 5cm. Bring to the boil over high heat. Simmer for 5 minutes, using a spoon to remove any scum that rises to the top. Add the onion, garlic, and bay leaves. Cover and turn the heat down to medium.

Toast the cumin seeds in a small pan over medium heat for 1 to 2 minutes, until fragrant. Grind in a mortar and pestle, and then add to the beans. Stir in the smoked paprika, oregano, chilli flakes, and allspice. Cover, turn the heat down to a simmer, and cook for 30 minutes.

Stir in the tomato purée, stock, olive oil, and a generous grind of black pepper. Continue to cook over medium-low heat for 1 hour, or until the beans are completely soft and beginning to melt together. Taste and adjust the seasoning. Depending on how salty your stock was, you may need to add salt.

Add the additional 2 cups just-boiled water into the pot and mash half of the beans until they thicken the soup. I use a potato masher for this, but you could also use the back of a wooden spoon.

To serve, ladle the soup into bowls and top with some or all the accompaniments: a swirl of soured cream or yoghurt, avocado tossed with a bit of lime juice, radish slices, a sprinkle of coriander, and/or jalapeño or chilli flakes.

Spinach and Kale Soup
with Crispy Chickpeas

SERVES 4

Green soups have a unique ability to make you feel like you are doing something good for yourself. This soup is a clever way to use up any leafy vegetables that are past their prime, so feel free to substitute whatever you might have at the back of your fridge, such as spring greens, rocket, or chard, for the spinach and kale. Make the crispy chickpeas in double or triple batches as they can be used for all kinds of soup and salad toppings, including my wedge salad (page 67).

CRISPY CHICKPEAS

1 (400g) tin chickpeas, drained and rinsed

2 tablespoons olive oil

1 teaspoon ground cumin

½ teaspoon sweet paprika

Salt

SOUP

Vegetable oil or butter

1 onion, roughly chopped

4 garlic cloves, crushed

1 teaspoon ground cumin

1 teaspoon ground coriander

Generous pinch ground nutmeg

1 medium potato, chopped

500ml vegetable stock

250ml water

200g spinach

200g kale

80ml whole milk or plant-based milk

2 tablespoons extra-virgin olive oil

Salt and freshly ground black pepper

To make the crispy chickpeas, preheat the oven to 200°C/ Fan 180°C/Gas Mark 6. Line a large baking sheet with foil or baking paper.

Toss the chickpeas with the olive oil, cumin, paprika, and ¼ teaspoon salt on the prepared baking sheet until well combined. Bake for 20 to 25 minutes, until crisp and golden.

While the chickpeas are baking, make the soup. Heat 2 tablespoons vegetable oil or butter in a large saucepan over medium heat. Add the onion and garlic and sauté for 4 minutes. Add the cumin, coriander, and nutmeg and stir everything together. Add the potato, stock, and water, cover, and cook for 10 minutes, or until the potato is soft. Add the spinach, kale, and ½ teaspoon pepper and cook for 5 to 6 minutes, until the greens have cooked.

Remove from the heat and stir in the milk and extra-virgin olive oil, then blend the soup until it is as smooth as you like it. Taste and adjust your seasoning – depending on how salty your stock is, you may want to add ½ teaspoon salt. To serve, ladle the soup into bowls and scatter over the crispy chickpeas.

Gazpacho

SERVES 4

- 1kg ripe tomatoes, quartered
- 1 large red pepper, roughly chopped
- 1 medium cucumber, peeled and cut into large chunks
- 2 tablespoons finely chopped red onion
- 3 garlic cloves, lightly smashed
- 100ml extra-virgin olive oil
- 1½ tablespoons red wine vinegar
- 1 tablespoon lemon juice
- Salt

The Iberian peninsula is my favourite region in Europe, and in my twenties I would visit each year, drawn to the mountains, Moorish architecture, and magnificent seas. The food of the various and diverse regions in Spain and Portugal was also a major draw (I'm a sucker for any country with good-quality olive oil, ripe figs, and saffron), but I rarely incorporated the dishes I ate into my culinary repertoire, as I feared the sun-kissed produce couldn't be replicated in damp, cold England. The exception to this is chilled summer soups such as gazpacho, which I make often in the height of summer as a refreshing and energising drink to snack on throughout the day. My version is purposely streamlined for speed, but depending on the quality of your food processor or how smooth you like your gazpacho, you can also run it through a sieve before serving, which results in a silkier texture. This tastes even better the next day, so it's especially handy to make ahead if you know it's going to be a scorcher tomorrow!

Combine the tomatoes, pepper, cucumber, onion, and garlic in a food processor or blender. Add the oil and blend until completely smooth. Transfer to a large bowl or jug, add the vinegar, lemon juice, and ¾ teaspoon salt, and stir well. If you like, you can run it through a sieve at this stage. Cover and refrigerate for at least 3 hours. Taste and adjust the seasoning before serving.

Ajo Blanco

SERVES 4

100g crustless white bread (slightly stale is fine)
1 litre water
200g blanched almonds
2 fat garlic cloves, peeled
Extra-virgin olive oil
3 tablespoons sherry vinegar or red wine vinegar, or more to taste
1 handful green grapes, chilled and halved
Salt

Spain's second most famous chilled soup doesn't get the recognition it deserves. Made with ground almonds, it manages to feel creamy yet somehow deceptively light and serves as an elegant start to a summer meal, ladled into small bowls and topped with chilled grapes. Traditionally this is prepared with sherry vinegar, so if you have that at home feel free to use it, but red wine vinegar works just as well. A little goes a long way here, as the ingredients are quite rich, so serve this in small bowls or cups. (See the photo on page 135.)

In a medium bowl, soak the bread in 500ml of the water for 10 minutes.

In a blender, combine the almonds and another 250ml water. Take the bread from the bowl, squeeze with your hands to remove the excess liquid, then roughly tear and add to the blender with the soaking water. Blend for 1 to 2 minutes, until finely ground.

With the blender running, slowly add the remaining 250ml water, garlic, 120ml oil, vinegar, and salt. Blend until completely smooth. Cover and refrigerate for at least 3 hours.

When you are ready to serve, taste and adjust the seasoning and acidity to your preference – you may want to add a touch more vinegar or salt. Divide into small bowls or cups, scatter the grape halves on top of the soup, and finish with a drizzle of oil.

Red Lentil and Tomato Soup
with Coriander Yoghurt

SERVES 4

2 tablespoons vegetable oil
1 medium onion, finely chopped
4 garlic cloves, crushed
1 large handful coriander, stems and leaves separated, finely chopped
2 teaspoons ground cumin
1½ teaspoons ground coriander
½ teaspoon Aleppo pepper or other mild chilli flakes
¼ teaspoon ground cinnamon
750ml vegetable stock
350ml just-boiled water
280g red lentils, rinsed
1 (400g) tin chopped tomatoes
Extra-virgin olive oil
125g Greek-style yoghurt or plant-based yoghurt
Salt and freshly ground black pepper

When I think of comforting soups, this is what comes to mind – a hearty lentil soup, which calls for being eaten on the sofa, under a blanket, on a chilly day. It's made from mostly pantry ingredients and takes very little effort so is perfect for those days when one's energy for cooking is somewhat limited. You can play around with the spices to suit your tastes – if you like more heat, a few more chilli flakes might work for you, or a pinch of smoked paprika.

Heat the vegetable oil in a large saucepan over medium heat. Add the onion and cook for 12 minutes, or until soft. Add the garlic, coriander stems, cumin, ground coriander, chilli flakes, and cinnamon and cook for another 2 minutes. Pour in the stock, just-boiled water, and lentils and stir well, then cover and cook for 10 minutes.

Add the tomatoes, ½ teaspoon salt, and ¼ teaspoon black pepper and cook for another 10 to 15 minutes, until the lentils are completely soft. Remove from the heat. If you prefer your soup smooth, blend it now. Then stir in 2 tablespoons olive oil. Taste and adjust the seasoning, adding more salt and pepper if needed.

Mix the coriander leaves with the yoghurt in a small bowl. To serve, ladle the soup into bowls and top with a spoonful of the herbed yoghurt and an extra drizzle of olive oil.

Yoghurt and Cucumber Soup

SERVES 4 TO 6

50g walnuts
500g Greek-style yoghurt
400ml cold water
200g finely diced Persian or regular cucumbers
3 tablespoons chopped dill
3 tablespoons chopped mint
1½ teaspoons dried mint
3 tablespoons raisins
Ice cubes, for serving
Dried edible rose petals, for serving (optional, but very pretty)
Sea salt flakes and freshly ground black pepper

As the heat of the summer ramps up, this luscious chilled yoghurt soup, packed with fresh and dried mint, is an incredibly refreshing and cooling starter that makes me feel like I'm taking a dip in the cold mountainous streams of northern Iran. It's one of those dishes that is initially met with some scepticism (yoghurt soup? cold? with just cucumber?), which is all the more reason that I encourage people to try it, often finding they come back for a second helping. This soup is best made with Persian cucumbers, which are smaller, sweeter, and more intensely flavoured, but regular cucumbers work fine too – just peel them first. Be sure to use full-fat Greek-style yoghurt (not strained or low-fat), and I prefer to use sea salt flakes as they have a more pronounced mineral flavour. You can find edible dried rose petals in Iranian supermarkets or online; they aren't essential, but a small pinch does make this soup take on a more elegant quality. This soup keeps in the fridge for about 24 hours.

Toast the walnuts in a small frying pan over medium heat for 1 to 2 minutes, stirring, until glossy. Roughly chop and set aside.

In a large bowl, whisk together the yoghurt and water. Stir in the cucumbers, fresh and dried herbs, raisins, toasted walnuts, 1½ teaspoons sea salt flakes and a generous grind of black pepper. Cover and refrigerate for at least 1 hour.

To serve, pour into cups or small bowls and add ice cubes and a pinch of rose petals, if using.

Mushroom and Buckwheat Soup

SERVES 4

- 2 tablespoons vegetable oil
- 1 medium onion, diced
- 4 garlic cloves, minced
- 2 celery stalks, diced
- 1 large carrot, peeled and diced
- 600g mixed mushrooms, thickly chopped
- 120g buckwheat groats
- 1 teaspoon dried oregano
- ½ teaspoon ground white pepper
- ½ teaspoon Aleppo pepper or other mild chilli flakes
- 700ml mushroom stock
- 250ml just-boiled water
- 1 tablespoon butter
- 60ml whole milk or plant-based milk
- 100g spinach leaves
- Finely grated Parmesan cheese, for serving

This soup is a recent discovery from my last trip to Istanbul, when I stopped by a neighbourhood café for a light dinner and was served a remarkable chicken soup that had been enhanced by the creaminess of sweet, nutty buckwheat. Back in my London kitchen, I replaced the poultry with a medley of mushrooms, which complement buckwheat's earthiness perfectly and conjure up the feeling of autumnal walks in a forest. Despite having "wheat" in its name, buckwheat isn't a grain but a seed and therefore gluten-free. You can find it in most supermarkets. If you haven't cooked with it before, you should bear in mind that its cooking time can vary based on the size of the seeds and their age. I recommend checking your pot after 15 minutes and adjusting the cooking time accordingly. You want the buckwheat to be chewy but still have some bite.

Heat the oil in a large saucepan over medium heat. Add the onion and fry for about 8 minutes. Add the garlic, celery, and carrot and cook for 2 minutes. Add the mushrooms and cook for another 5 minutes, stirring frequently.

Mix in the buckwheat, oregano, white pepper, chilli flakes, stock, just-boiled water, and butter. Cover, turn the heat down to low, and simmer for 15 to 20 minutes, until the buckwheat is soft.

Stir in the milk and spinach, bring to a simmer, and cook until the spinach wilts, about 3 minutes. Taste and adjust the seasoning, adding a bit more water to loosen, depending on how thick you like your soup.

To serve, ladle into bowls and top with grated Parmesan.

Spiced Parsnip Soup
with Dukkah

SERVES 4

2 tablespoons butter
1 medium onion
3 garlic cloves, finely grated
600g parsnips, peeled and cut into small chunks
300g carrots, peeled and cut into small chunks
300g potato, peeled and cut into small chunks
2 teaspoons ras el hanout
750ml vegetable or chicken stock
250ml just-boiled water
Salt and freshly ground black pepper

TOPPINGS

Greek-style yoghurt
Dukkah (recipe follows)
Extra-virgin olive oil

The sweetness of parsnips is the perfect pairing for the North African spice mix ras el hanout. This widely available blend combines ground cumin, cinnamon, coriander, turmeric, ginger, cardamom, and sometimes rose petals to fill your kitchen with intoxicating sweet scents and add punch to stews, soups, and marinades. Here I've paired it with dukkah, an Egyptian nut and spice condiment that makes a fragrant and nutty topping. I've included a recipe for it on the following page, but it's also very easy to source in most larger supermarkets or online.

Melt the butter in a large saucepan over medium heat. Add the onion and sauté for 5 minutes, or until soft. Add the garlic, parsnips, carrots, potato, ras el hanout, and ½ teaspoon salt and stir well. Sweat the vegetables for 10 minutes, stirring frequently to ensure the vegetables don't brown – you are looking to evaporate their water, which will condense their flavour.

Add the stock and just-boiled water, cover, and cook until the vegetables are soft, about 15 minutes. Blend the soup until smooth.

To serve, ladle into small bowls and top with a spoonful of yoghurt, a generous sprinkle of dukkah, and a drizzle of olive oil.

Dukkah

- 85g hazelnuts, finely chopped
- 2 tablespoons sesame seeds
- 2 tablespoons coriander seeds
- 1 tablespoon cumin seeds
- Salt and freshly ground black pepper

In a small frying pan, toast the hazelnuts, sesame seeds, coriander seeds, and cumin seeds over low heat for 2 to 3 minutes, until the nuts turn glossy and fragrant. Remove from the heat and stir in ¼ teaspoon salt and a generous grind of pepper. Dukkah will keep in an airtight container for about 1 week.

The Main Event

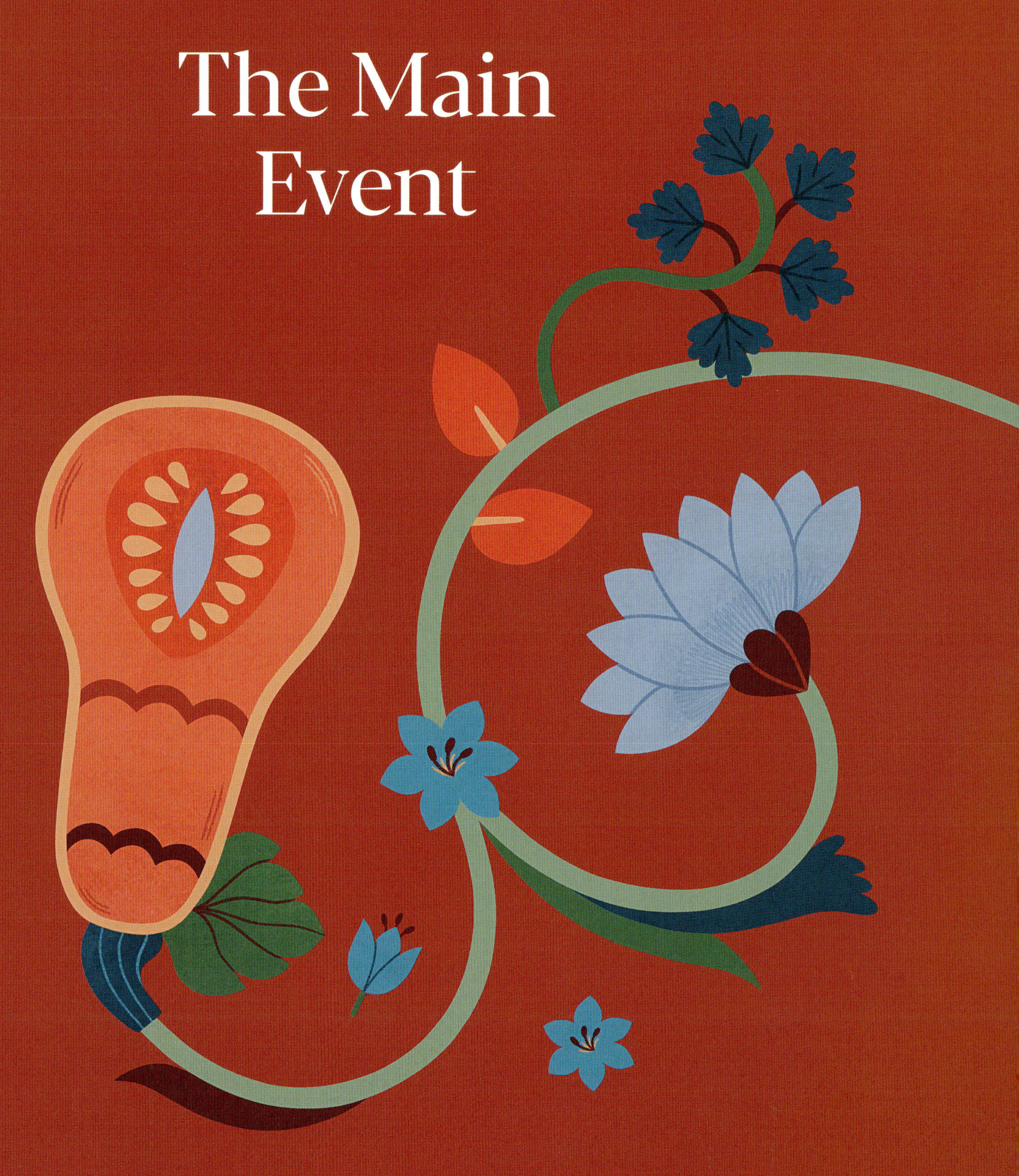

*After a good dinner one can forgive anybody,
even one's own relations.*
– **OSCAR WILDE**

As I've transitioned to incorporating more plant-based eating in my diet, it's been hugely important to me to be able to continue to enjoy and share the dishes I grew up on with friends and family members who don't eat meat or fish. So in this chapter you'll find vegetarian and vegan versions of classic Persian dishes, and I can happily testify that these adaptations are as tasty as the traditional versions (and even more importantly for me, spark the same memories from my taste buds). From ambrosial khoreshts made with saffron and dried limes to creamy daals spiked with coconut milk and curry leaves to quick weeknight pasta recipes and special occasion showstoppers, there's something for everyone in this diverse chapter, a celebration of how plant-based eating can be hearty, packed with flavour, and utterly satisfying.

Persian Aubergine, Split Pea, and Dried Lime Stew (Gheimeh Badinjan)

SERVES 4 TO 6

200g yellow split peas
3 large aubergines, cut into long, thick wedges
Vegetable oil
2 medium onions, finely chopped
4 garlic cloves, finely chopped
1¼ teaspoons cumin seeds
1¼ teaspoons coriander seeds
1 teaspoon ground turmeric
¼ teaspoon ground cinnamon
¼ teaspoon ground white pepper
¼ teaspoon Aleppo pepper or other mild chilli flakes
500ml just-boiled water
500ml vegetable stock
3 tablespoons tomato purée
4 dried limes
1 tablespoon lemon juice, or more to taste
Pinch saffron strands
Pinch sugar
Fried Potato Topping (recipe follows, optional)
Salt

Dried limes are a quintessential Iranian ingredient and the scent of my childhood. They adorn several of Iran's most popular stews, imparting a wonderfully citrusy and slightly bitter base note, and are widely available online, in larger supermarkets, or in Middle Eastern supermarkets. Their skins are quite sharp and bitter, and while I love them, you may want to avoid them if you are eating this for the first time. I've included a fried potato topping, which I always make if serving this for guests or special occasions, but for everyday cooking you can leave it out – it's not an essential component. As with all Iranian stews, the flavours improve the next day, and this keeps well in the fridge for up to 3 days. Serve with Persian Rice with Saffron Tahdig (page 153) or regular steamed rice, and of course an Everyday Middle Eastern Chopped Salad (page 85). (See the photo on page 147.)

Rinse the split peas and soak in a large bowl of cold water for at least 6 hours.

Preheat the oven to 200°C/Fan 180°C/Gas Mark 6. Line a large baking sheet with baking paper.

Arrange the aubergine wedges on the prepared baking sheet. Pour 4 tablespoons of vegetable oil into a small bowl and use a pastry brush to coat each side of the aubergine before sprinkling them with ½ teaspoon salt. Roast for 25 minutes, or until completely soft and cooked through. Set aside.

Meanwhile, heat 3 tablespoons vegetable oil in a large saucepan over medium heat. Add the onions and cook for 15 minutes, stirring occasionally, until brown and soft. Add the garlic and cook for a few minutes, adding a bit more oil or water if the pan has dried out.

Toast the cumin and coriander seeds in a small pan over medium heat for 1 or 2 minutes, stirring a few times, until fragrant. Transfer to a mortar and pestle or spice grinder and grind. Add the spices to the onions, along with the turmeric, cinnamon, white pepper, and chilli flakes and stir well.

Drain the split peas and add to the onions, along with 500ml of the just-boiled water. Bring to the boil, using a spoon to remove any scum that rises to the surface. Cover and cook over medium heat for 15 minutes. Add the stock, tomato purée, and 1 teaspoon salt.

Pierce each dried lime with a fork a few times and add these to the pot along with the lemon juice.

Grind the saffron and sugar in a mortar and pestle. Add 2 tablespoons just-boiled water and let steep for 5 minutes, then add to the stew. Cover and simmer until the split peas are completely cooked and soft. Depending on the age and freshness of the split peas, this can take anywhere from 20 to 40 minutes (you may need to add a touch more water if they dry out).

Once the split peas are cooked, gently stir in the aubergine. Cook for 5 minutes to bring everything together. Taste and adjust the seasoning to your preference – you may want a touch more salt, black pepper, or lemon juice. Just before serving, top the stew with the fried potatoes, if using.

Fried Potato Topping

Vegetable oil
1 medium potato, peeled and cut into thin fries
Salt

Line a plate with a few sheets of kitchen paper. Heat 5 tablespoons oil in a large frying pan over medium heat. Add the potato, sprinkle with ½ teaspoon salt, and cook until crisp on the outside and soft within, 5 to 8 minutes. You may want to work in batches so that you don't crowd the pan. Transfer the fries to the lined plate to drain.

Persian Rice
with Saffron Tahdig

SERVES 6

400g white basmati rice
¼ teaspoon saffron strands
Pinch sugar
3 tablespoons just-boiled water
65g yoghurt (optional)
45g butter
2 tablespoons vegetable oil
Salt

Nothing says "wow factor" more than bringing a plate of Persian rice with a crispy, buttery, saffron-infused crust (called tahdig) to the table. There's an art to cooking Persian rice, as it's a unique technique and takes a bit of trial and error as you work out how to identify the different steps, but once you crack it, there is no looking back. If for some reason it doesn't come out right the first time, you can simply serve it as a bowl of rice and no one will be any wiser! There is no specific water-to-rice ratio with this method, so you can adapt the recipe to cook any amount of rice by following the instructions below. Just be sure to use a heavy, nonstick pan with a snug-fitting lid and have a clean tea towel or some kitchen paper on hand for lining the lid. The yoghurt isn't essential but helps the rice grains bind together better for the tahdig.

Rinse the rice under cold running water until the water runs clear, then let soak in a bowl of cold water for 15 minutes.

Grind the saffron with the sugar in a mortar and pestle, then add the just-boiled water and let steep for 5 minutes.

Bring a large pot of water to the boil and add 2 tablespoons salt (don't worry that it will be too salty – the rice won't absorb much of this as it is only in the water for a short time). Add the rice and boil for 6 to 7 minutes, until the rice is al dente and half-cooked. You can test this by having a bite; you want it to be soft on the outside but still a bit firm in the middle. Drain the rice and rinse it with cold water.

If you are using the yoghurt, mix it with 75g of the cooked rice.

continues ►

In a medium saucepan, heat 30g of the butter, the oil, and a pinch of salt over medium heat. Add 1 tablespoon of the saffron liquid. When the oil is bubbling hot, gently layer the yoghurt rice (if using) or 75g of the plain cooked rice over the bottom of the pan. Spoon the remaining rice gently into the pan, ladle by ladle. You want to keep some air between the grains so they can stay separate while cooking, so don't just throw it all in but rather gently layer the rice into a pyramid shape.

Use the end of a wooden spoon to make four deep holes in the rice. Cut the remaining 15g of butter into bits and scatter them on top, along with the rest of the saffron liquid.

Place some kitchen paper or a clean tea towel on top of the pan and place the lid on tightly. Cook for 5 minutes over medium heat, then turn the heat down low and cook for 15 minutes. Do not be tempted to sneak a peek as it will spoil the cooking process! Take the pan off the heat and let stand, still covered, for 2 minutes.

Fill the sink with a little cold water and place the pan in it, with the lid still tightly on. The cold water will produce a rush of steam inside the pan, which will release the crispy base.

Remove the lid and place a large plate over the pan. Quickly and deftly turn it over and voilà! You should have a beautiful, golden Persian rice cake.

Ghormeh Sabzi
with Mushrooms

SERVES 4

Vegetable oil
1 medium onion, finely chopped
4 garlic cloves, finely grated
30g coriander stems and leaves, finely chopped
30g parsley stems and leaves, finely chopped
30g chives, finely chopped
50g ghormeh sabzi dried herb blend
1 teaspoon ground turmeric
500ml vegetable stock
250ml just-boiled water
2 (400g) tins red kidney beans, drained and rinsed
2 tablespoons extra-virgin olive oil
1 tablespoon soy sauce or tamari
4 dried limes
1 tablespoon lime juice, or more to taste
250g oyster mushrooms, separated into individual mushrooms
15g butter
Salt and freshly ground black pepper

There are few dishes that epitomise Iranian cuisine and its love of herbs more than ghormeh sabzi, a traditional khoresht packed with mixed greens and dried limes. I would go so far as to say that this is probably Iran's national dish, and each home has their own version of it, featuring their favourite combination of herbs, chopped and fried down as an intense base for this aromatic stew. My vegetarian version uses thick strips of oyster mushrooms instead of lamb and a combination of fresh and dried herbs to reduce the prep and cooking time. You can easily source ghormeh sabzi herb blends online or at any Iranian supermarket. As dried limes can have quite a pungent taste when eaten whole, you may wish to put them to one side before eating; I adore the sour hit, but it's not for everyone! This tastes best after it's been left to sit for a few hours or, even better, overnight. Serve with Persian Rice with Saffron Tahdig (page 153) or steamed rice with an Everyday Middle Eastern Chopped Salad (page 85) on the side. (See the photo on page 157.)

Heat 2 tablespoons vegetable oil in a large saucepan over medium heat. Add the onion and cook for about 15 minutes, until softened, then add the garlic and cook for 2 minutes. Add the coriander, parsley, and chives and cook for about 6 minutes, stirring often, until most of their water has evaporated and they are darker in colour.

Add the dried herb blend, turmeric, stock, just-boiled water, kidney beans, olive oil, soy sauce, and ½ teaspoon pepper. Pierce each dried lime a few times with a fork and then add these, along with the lime juice. Turn the heat down to low, cover, and simmer for 25 minutes.

continues ▶

Heat 2 tablespoons vegetable oil in a frying pan over medium heat. Add the mushrooms, in batches if necessary, along with a generous pinch of salt, and cook until golden and crispy, about 5 minutes. Transfer to a plate.

After the stew has cooked, press each dried lime against the side of the pot so that they burst, then stir well. You can now remove the limes if you don't want to eat them.

Stir in the butter and simmer for 2 to 3 minutes, until the stew has thickened. Fold in the mushrooms. Cook for a final 3 minutes to bring everything together. Taste and adjust for seasoning, adding a bit more salt, pepper, or lime juice to your preference.

Mung Daal

SERVES 4 WITH RICE AND ACCOMPANIMENTS

- 300g yellow split mung daal
- 1.2 litres just-boiled water
- 1½ teaspoons garam masala, or more to taste
- ½ teaspoon ground turmeric
- 2 tablespoons vegetable oil
- 2 fat garlic cloves, finely grated
- 1 heaped tablespoon finely grated ginger
- 1½ teaspoons cumin seeds
- 2 tablespoons extra-virgin olive oil, coconut oil, or ghee
- ¼ teaspoon chilli flakes, or more to taste
- Chopped coriander, for garnish (optional)
- Salt and freshly ground black pepper

This is my everyday daal recipe, on weekly rotation in my house. I always make it with yellow split mung daal as it's the most digestible pulse and is heralded for its gut-friendly properties in Ayurvedic cooking, but you could also use red lentils if that's what you have on hand. Serve with basmati rice, a good lime or mango pickle, and a sharp, chopped salad on the side (page 85). This freezes well, so store it ahead for those days when you don't have the time or inclination to cook.

Rinse the split mung daal in cold water, then let soak in a bowl of cold water for 30 minutes.

Drain the mung daal and transfer to a large saucepan. Top with the just-boiled water and bring to the boil over high heat, skimming off any white scum with a spoon. Turn the heat down to medium, add the garam masala and turmeric, cover, and cook until completely soft. You can tell the daal is ready when the mung daal have broken up and are blending into each other; depending on their age and freshness, this can take anywhere from 20 to 40 minutes.

Meanwhile, heat the vegetable oil in a frying pan over medium-low heat. Add the garlic and ginger and cook for 3 minutes. Add the cumin seeds and cook, stirring well, until they are lightly toasted and fragrant, 1 to 2 minutes. Remove the pan from the heat.

When the daal is ready, add the spiced garlic and ginger mixture, along with the olive oil, 1 teaspoon salt, ¼ teaspoon black pepper, and the chilli flakes. Stir well, cover, and cook for 5 minutes to bring everything together.

Taste and adjust the seasoning, adding a touch more salt, chilli flakes, or garam masala if you want. Serve with a sprinkle of coriander if using.

Smoky Chickpeas
with Orzo and Cavolo Nero

SERVES 4

Vegetable oil
4 garlic cloves, minced
2 (400g) tins chickpeas, drained and rinsed
500ml vegetable stock
2 teaspoons dried oregano
1 teaspoon Aleppo pepper or other mild chilli flakes
½ teaspoon smoked sweet paprika
350g orzo
500ml just-boiled water
3 tablespoons tomato purée
30g butter
200g cavolo nero or any other greens, shredded
Extra-virgin olive oil
Salt and freshly ground black pepper

PANGRATTATO
Vegetable oil
Grated zest of 1 lemon
2 garlic cloves, finely grated
60g breadcrumbs
4 tablespoons finely chopped parsley, chives, and/or coriander
Salt

It was on a trip to Rome as a teenager that I first ate the winning Italian combination of chickpeas cooked with small rounds of pasta. I can still picture the small blue-and-white patterned bowl from which I greedily devoured it. Many years later I came to know the dish as pasta e ceci, and years later still I would make my own riff on a chickpea and pasta stew, not in the least bit traditional but bringing together elements of soft beans, chewy pasta, and an abundance of Mediterranean seasonings. You can replace the cavolo nero (aka lacinato kale) with any other robust green of your choice. If you are using jarred chickpeas (which is what I most commonly do) or if you have cooked the beans from scratch, you won't need to cook them for more than 10 minutes, but some varieties of tinned chickpeas (especially in the UK) can take up to 30 to 40 minutes to soften, so I always feel I need to give that warning! I like to add a topping of pangrattato (fried breadcrumbs), but you can skip it and stick with grated Parmesan if you prefer.

Heat 2 tablespoons vegetable oil in a large saucepan over low heat. Add the garlic and cook for 2 minutes, stirring often so it doesn't burn. Add the chickpeas, stock, oregano, chilli flakes, and paprika and stir well. Cook for 5 minutes, then taste the chickpeas; if they are of the harder variety, cook until they have completely softened.

Once the chickpeas are plump and soft, add the orzo, just-boiled water, tomato purée, and butter. Stir well, cover, and simmer for 5 minutes. Add the cavolo nero and cook for 8 to 10 minutes, stirring occasionally to keep the stew from sticking to the bottom of the pan. Taste to adjust the seasoning; depending

continues ▶

on how salty your stock is, you may want to add more salt and/or some black pepper.

While the greens are cooking, make the pangrattato. Heat 2 tablespoons vegetable oil in a small frying pan over low heat. Add the lemon zest and garlic and cook for 2 minutes, stirring often. Add the breadcrumbs, herbs, and ¼ teaspoon salt and keep stirring until the breadcrumbs have turned slightly golden. Transfer the breadcrumbs to a small bowl so they don't burn.

Once the orzo and greens have cooked, taste the stew and adjust the seasoning. You may want to add a bit more water to loosen the stew if it's thick. Ladle into a serving dish, top with the fried breadcrumbs, and drizzle with olive oil.

Squash, Lentil, and Apricot Stew

SERVES 6

- 350g butternut squash, peeled and cut into small cubes (about 2.5cm)
- Vegetable oil
- 1 medium onion, finely chopped
- 2 celery stalks, finely chopped
- 4 fat garlic cloves, finely grated
- 1½ teaspoons ground cumin
- 1½ teaspoons ground coriander
- 1 teaspoon smoked sweet paprika
- ½ teaspoon ground cinnamon
- ½ teaspoon ground ginger
- ¼ teaspoon Aleppo pepper or other mild chilli flakes
- 170g red lentils, rinsed
- 700ml plus 2 tablespoons just-boiled water
- ¼ teaspoon saffron strands
- Pinch sugar
- 1 (400g) tin chickpeas, drained and rinsed
- 1 (400g) tin chopped tomatoes
- 500ml chicken or vegetable stock
- 45g white basmati rice
- 8 dried apricots, halved
- 1 handful coriander leaves, chopped, plus more for garnish
- 3 tablespoons extra-virgin olive oil
- 2 tablespoons lemon juice, plus more to taste
- Salt and freshly ground black pepper

Sitting somewhere between a soup and a stew, this nourishing one-pot meal takes inspiration from the Moroccan soup harira but adds butternut squash and dried apricots, cooked in the heady sweet spices of cinnamon, ginger, paprika, and saffron. I have an unfashionable tendency to cook vegetables until they are exceptionally soft and particularly like to do this for this soup, relishing in watching the orange chunks of butternut squash and apricots disintegrate into the broth, which lends it a more viscous and velvety texture. Serve with buttered sourdough toast or flatbreads drizzled with extra-virgin olive oil. The flavours improve after the stew has rested overnight, and it also freezes well so is ideal for batch-cooking. **(See the photo on page 165.)**

Preheat the oven to 200°C/Fan 180°C/Gas Mark 6.

On a large baking sheet, toss the butternut squash in a couple tablespoons vegetable oil. Sprinkle with ¼ teaspoon salt and a generous grind of black pepper. Roast for 15 to 20 minutes, until just cooked through but still firm.

Heat 2 tablespoons vegetable oil in a large saucepan over medium heat. Add the onion and sauté until softened, stirring occasionally, about 10 minutes. Add the celery, garlic, cumin, coriander, paprika, cinnamon, ginger, and chilli flakes, reduce the heat to low, and cook for 5 minutes. Add the lentils and 700ml of the just-boiled water, cover, and cook until softened, about 12 minutes.

Meanwhile, grind the saffron and sugar in a mortar and pestle. Add the remaining 2 tablespoons just-boiled water and allow to steep for 5 minutes.

continues ▶

When the lentils are soft, add the saffron liquid, chickpeas, tomatoes, stock, rice, ½ teaspoon salt, and ½ teaspoon pepper and stir to combine. Cover, turn the heat down to medium-low, and simmer, stirring occasionally, for 30 minutes. Add more water if the stew is dry.

Add the squash, apricots, coriander, olive oil, and lemon juice and cook for another 5 minutes, or until the squash is beginning to melt into the stew. Taste and season as needed. Depending on how salty your stock is, you may want to add more salt, and it would definitely benefit from a generous grind of black pepper. Serve garnished with more coriander, if you like, and a sprinkle of chilli flakes.

Persian Celery and Bean Stew (Khoresht-e Karafs)

SERVES 4

Vegetable oil
1 medium onion, finely chopped
4 garlic cloves, finely grated
1 teaspoon ground turmeric
½ teaspoon ground coriander
½ teaspoon ground cumin
½ teaspoon ground white pepper
100g parsley, finely chopped
55g mint leaves, finely chopped
400g celery, cut diagonally into small pieces
2 (400g) tins borlotti beans, drained and rinsed
500ml vegetable stock
Juice of 1 lime, plus more to taste
3 tablespoons extra-virgin olive oil
Salt

There is so much brightness and aroma to be found in celery's elegant stalks. It's truly one of our most underused and underrated vegetables, and I always enjoy making this stew for any celery sceptics. As in so many Persian dishes, large bunches of parsley and mint are cooked down to create a fragrant base, which normally then is mixed with lamb but here I've substituted speckled borlotti beans. Also, like all Iranian stews, this a good dish to make ahead of time; it will taste best after sitting for a few hours and improves considerably when eaten the next day. Serve with Persian Rice with Saffron Tahdig (page 153) or simple steamed white rice and an Everyday Middle Eastern Chopped Salad (page 85), plus some yoghurt on the side.

Heat 2 tablespoons vegetable oil in a large saucepan over medium heat. Add the onion and cook for 20 minutes, until soft and translucent. Add the garlic, turmeric, coriander, cumin, and white pepper and cook for 2 minutes. Add 1 tablespoon vegetable oil and then the parsley, mint, and celery and cook for 10 minutes, stirring often to evaporate most of their water. Add the beans, stock, and ¾ teaspoon salt, cover, and simmer for 20 minutes, or until the celery is very soft.

Add the lime juice and olive oil and cook for 2 minutes. Taste and adjust the seasoning as needed, including adding another squeeze of lime juice if you think it needs a touch more sharpness – Iranian food embraces the sour taste, so I'm always adding a bit more, but just go with what you prefer. Set aside for at least 1 hour before serving.

Chickpeas

with Sweet Potatoes and Avocado Smash

SERVES 4

600g sweet potatoes, peeled and cut into small chunks
Vegetable oil
1 medium onion, finely chopped
4 garlic cloves, minced
2 tablespoons minced ginger
2 teaspoons ground cumin
1 teaspoon ground coriander
½ teaspoon ground allspice
½ teaspoon Aleppo pepper or other mild chilli flakes
2 (400g) tins chopped tomatoes
1 (400g) tin chickpeas, drained and rinsed
350ml just-boiled water
150g shredded kale
Extra-virgin olive oil
Salt and freshly ground black pepper

SMASHED AVOCADOS

2 ripe Hass avocados
2 tablespoons lemon juice
Extra-virgin olive oil
1 small handful coriander leaves
Salt and freshly ground black pepper

This wonderfully versatile stew can be spooned over rice for dinner, spread over toasted and buttered sourdough for lunch, or eaten as part of a weekend brunch along with some poached eggs. It keeps well in the fridge for a few days, and the flavours will improve with time, but if you are making it ahead of time, leave making the smashed avocado until just before you are serving. Cooking times will vary depending on the brand of chickpeas you use. I tend to use jarred chickpeas or cook them from scratch (see page 27), but if you are using tinned chickpeas, especially from UK supermarkets, some brands can take 30 minutes to soften. Just keep an eye on their cooking and tweak the time accordingly; you want the chickpeas to feel so soft that they can easily be pressed with the back of a fork and melt into the sauce.

Preheat the oven to 200°C/Fan 180°C/Gas Mark 6.

On a large baking sheet, toss the sweet potatoes with 2 tablespoons vegetable oil and ½ teaspoon salt. Roast until soft, about 20 minutes, flipping them halfway through to ensure even cooking.

Meanwhile, heat 2 tablespoons vegetable oil in a large saucepan over medium-low heat. Add the onion and cook for about 15 minutes, until soft. Add the garlic, ginger, cumin, ground coriander, allspice, and chilli flakes and cook for 2 minutes. Add the tomatoes, chickpeas, 1 teaspoon salt, ½ teaspoon black pepper, and the just-boiled water and stir well. Turn the heat down to low, cover, and simmer for 10 minutes.

continues ►

Add the kale, cover, and simmer until it has wilted, 5 to 10 minutes. You may need to add a touch more water if the stew is looking thick. Gently fold in the roasted sweet potatoes and 3 tablespoons olive oil. Taste and adjust the seasoning.

To make the avocado smash, combine the avocados, lemon juice, 2 tablespoons olive oil, coriander, ¼ teaspoon salt, and ¼ teaspoon pepper in a medium bowl and use the back of a fork to mash them into a chunky sauce. Serve alongside or on top of each portion of the stew.

Aubergine Fesenjan

SERVES 4

300g walnuts
1.2 litres cold water
5 ice cubes
120ml pomegranate molasses, plus more to taste
1½ tablespoons tomato purée
2 teaspoons sugar, plus more to taste
¾ teaspoon golpar
¼ teaspoon ground cinnamon
Salt and freshly ground black pepper

AUBERGINE

3 medium aubergines, cut into thick wedges
60ml olive oil
Salt

The Iranian festival of Yalda takes place on the winter solstice and is an evening spent sharing poetry and snacking on red fruits such as pomegranates, which symbolise the crimson hues of the sun rising after the longest night. Fesenjan, a sumptuous sweet-and-sour stew made with ground walnuts and pomegranate molasses, is often cooked for this celebration. It is cooked low and slow, and you can tell that it is ready when the nuts release their oils and you see a clear slick of oil sitting on top of the sauce. The timing is dependent on the variety of walnuts you use, so if you've reached the end of the suggested cooking time and the oils haven't released yet, give it another 30 minutes to an hour until they do. Golpar is an earthy, citrusy spice you can source online or in Iranian stores, though you can also make the dish without. Serve the stew with white rice, radishes, and an Everyday Middle Eastern Chopped salad (page 85) or a or a plate of Sabzi Khordan (page 110). (See the photo on page 173).

Grind the walnuts as finely as possible in a food processor. Add 200ml water and blend again until a smooth paste forms.

Transfer the walnuts to a large saucepan and pour over 1 litre cold water. Bring to the boil, then turn the heat down to a simmer. Stir until the walnut paste completely dissolves, then simmer, partially covered, for 2 hours. Stir occasionally to make sure the walnuts don't stick to the bottom.

Add the ice cubes and bring back to a simmer. Stir in the pomegranate molasses, tomato purée, sugar, golpar, cinnamon, 1 teaspoon salt, and a generous grind of pepper until well combined. Cover and cook for another 1½ hours, removing the lid for the last 30 minutes of cooking to allow the sauce to thicken.

continues ▶

Season to taste with more sugar (for sweet) or pomegranate molasses (for sour) – you want a balance of both.

While the walnuts are cooking, preheat the oven to 180°C/Fan 160°C/Gas Mark 4.

Arrange the aubergine on a large baking sheet, brush it with the olive oil, and season with ¾ teaspoon salt on both sides. Roast for 30 minutes, or until it is completely soft.

When the stew is ready, carefully transfer the roasted aubergine to the pan with the stew and heat through gently for 5 minutes.

Mung Bean, Spinach, and Tomato Daal

SERVES 4

200g whole mung beans
1.7 litres just-boiled water
1 jalapeño chilli, halved and deseeded
2 tablespoons vegetable oil
1 medium onion, diced
4 garlic cloves, crushed
1 heaped tablespoon finely chopped ginger
2 teaspoons garam masala
1½ teaspoons cumin seeds
1 teaspoon ground turmeric
¼ teaspoon cayenne pepper, or more to taste
3 tablespoons tomato purée
3 heaped tablespoons fenugreek leaves (kasoori methi)
300g frozen spinach
30g butter or ghee, or 2 tablespoons olive oil
Salt and freshly ground black pepper

A few years ago, while at a yoga retreat in Stroud, England, I stole away a few hours one afternoon, reading my teacher's wonderful assortment of cookbooks. I can't remember the book where I found a recipe for mung bean and fenugreek daal, but I do remember making a note of the ingredients as I thought it would be a winning combination. Soon after I returned home, I spent some time working up this recipe, which produces a deeply aromatic daal. I suggest using frozen spinach for ease and speed, but if you want to use fresh spinach, you'll need twice as much by weight. The fenugreek leaves (often labelled kasoori methi) give this dish its pungency, so don't skip them. You can find them in the international aisle of major supermarkets or in South Asian supermarkets or online. Serve with wholewheat flatbreads or rice, plus a tangy lime or mango pickle and yoghurt on the side.

Rinse the mung beans under cold running water, then put them in a large bowl of cold water with ½ teaspoon salt and set aside to soak for 1 hour.

Rinse and drain the beans and transfer to a large saucepan. Top with the just-boiled water and bring to a rolling boil over medium heat; boil for 5 minutes. Use a spoon to remove any scum that rises to the top, then add the jalapeño, cover, and cook for 20 minutes.

While the beans are cooking, heat the vegetable oil in a large frying pan over medium heat. Add the onion and cook for 15 minutes, or until soft. Add the garlic and ginger and cook for another 2 minutes. Stir in the garam masala, cumin seeds, turmeric, cayenne, 1 teaspoon salt, and ¼ teaspoon black pepper. Cook for 2 minutes, then transfer the mixture to the pot

continues ▶

of mung beans, along with the tomato purée and fenugreek leaves. Cover and cook for 15 minutes, or until the mung beans have softened (depending on the age of your beans, the timing can vary). You may need to add a bit more water if it starts to look dry.

Add the spinach and butter, cover, and cook, stirring every so often, until the leaves have wilted, 5 to 7 minutes. Taste and adjust the seasoning to your preference.

Curried Squash, Kale, and Bean Stew

SERVES 4

3 tablespoons vegetable oil
1 medium onion, finely chopped
4 garlic cloves, finely grated
1½ tablespoons finely grated ginger
2 teaspoons ground coriander
1 teaspoon ground cumin
1 teaspoon ground turmeric
¼ teaspoon cayenne pepper
600g butternut squash, peeled and cut into around 2cm cubes
2 (400g) tins white beans, drained and rinsed
1 (400ml) can full-fat coconut milk
250ml vegetable stock
1 tablespoon soy sauce or tamari
2 teaspoons maple syrup
125g shredded kale leaves
1 large handful coriander leaves, roughly chopped
Salt and freshly ground black pepper

When autumn days start turning darker and colder, I crave dishes such as this lightly spiced coconut stew, infused with citrusy notes from the coriander seeds and leaves. I love its flexibility – you can serve it with bread or steamed rice or add a splash more stock and eat as a thick soup. You can replace the squash with pumpkin or any other kind of winter squash and the kale with collard greens or spinach. Be sure to use full-fat coconut milk – as my oft-repeated mantra goes, what you lose in fat, you lose in taste.

Heat the oil in a large pan over medium heat. Add the onion and cook for 10 minutes, until soft. Add the garlic, ginger, ground coriander, cumin, turmeric, and cayenne and cook for a couple of minutes, stirring frequently.

Add the squash, beans, coconut milk, stock, soy sauce, maple syrup, 1 teaspoon salt, and ½ teaspoon black pepper and mix well. Cover and cook for 10 minutes or so, until the squash is tender but still has some bite.

In the meantime, cook the kale in a large pot of boiling water until it has cooked through, 5 to 7 minutes. Drain.

Once the squash is soft, stir in the kale and most of the coriander, reserving a small handful for garnish. Simmer for a minute, then taste and adjust the seasoning. Garnish with the reserved coriander and serve.

Creamy Mushroom, Tofu, and Kale Pasta

SERVES 4

2 tablespoons vegetable oil
1 medium leek, thinly sliced
4 garlic cloves, minced
400g brown mushrooms, thinly sliced
400g penne pasta
150g shredded kale
Salt

TOFU SAUCE

300g silken tofu
120ml water
1 tablespoon soy sauce or tamari
Grated zest of 1 lemon
3 tablespoons extra-virgin olive oil
3 tablespoons grated Parmesan cheese or nutritional yeast
Salt and freshly ground black pepper

FOR SERVING

Aleppo pepper or other mild chilli flakes
Grated Parmesan cheese or nutritional yeast
Freshly ground black pepper

If you want to avoid dairy but love creamy sauces, silken tofu can make a wonderful substitution, especially in pasta sauces, with the bonus of an extra protein hit. Feel free to substitute any greens you like for the kale; just amend the cooking time accordingly (winter kale is thicker, so it takes longer to cook than summer kale). You are looking for a soft texture to the cooked greens that isn't too chewy. Top with a sprinkle of chilli flakes and extra Parmesan or nutritional yeast.

Heat the vegetable oil in a large frying pan over medium heat. Add the leek and sauté for 10 minutes, or until soft. Add the garlic and cook for 2 minutes. Add the mushrooms and ½ teaspoon salt and cook for 8 to 10 minutes, stirring often, until the mushrooms are soft.

Fill a large saucepan with water, add 1 tablespoon salt, and bring to the boil. Add the pasta and cook according to the packet instructions until al dente.

While the pasta is cooking, fill another saucepan with just-boiled water, add the kale, and simmer over medium-high heat until soft, 5 to 8 minutes. Drain and squeeze out any excess water.

To make the tofu sauce, combine the tofu, water, soy sauce, lemon zest, olive oil, Parmesan, ½ teaspoon salt, and a generous grind of black pepper in a food processor (or in a medium bowl if using a hand blender) and process until smooth. Pour this thick sauce into the pan of mushrooms and leek, then stir in the kale.

When the pasta is ready, drain, reserving 120ml of the cooking water. Transfer the pasta to a serving bowl and stir in the sauce. Taste and adjust the seasoning to your preference, loosening the sauce with the reserved pasta water if it needs it – you are aiming for a rich, creamy sauce. Finish with a sprinkle of chilli flakes, lots of black pepper, and more Parmesan or nutritional yeast to taste.

Rajma (Punjabi Spiced Red Kidney Beans)

SERVES 4 WITH ACCOMPANIMENTS

- 2 tablespoons vegetable oil
- 1 small red onion, finely chopped
- 1 tablespoon finely grated ginger
- 3 garlic cloves, finely grated
- 1½ teaspoons garam masala
- 1 teaspoon ground cumin
- ½ teaspoon ground turmeric
- ¼ teaspoon cayenne pepper, plus more to taste
- 2 (400g) tins red kidney beans, drained and rinsed
- 2½ tablespoons tomato purée
- 250ml just-boiled water
- 2 tablespoons dried fenugreek leaves (kasoori methi)
- 30g butter or ghee
- 1 small handful coriander leaves
- Salt and freshly ground black pepper

There are few ingredients that transport me back to my family's kitchen more than fenugreek leaves, used by my Iranian mother extensively in Persian dishes such as Ghormeh Sabzi (page 155) and by my Pakistani father in Punjabi specialities, such as this spiced kidney bean dish. Fenugreek leaves are deeply pungent and slightly bitter, so you need only a small amount to pack a lot of punch. As I'm always looking for shortcuts midweek, I usually make this with jarred or tinned beans for a quick dinner that takes about 30 minutes to make from start to finish. This goes well with some steamed rice or flatbreads, South Asian achaar pickles, and a chopped tomato, cucumber, and red onion salad. If you have more time, you might want to make a Punjabi Spiced Vegetable Medley (page 111) to accompany it too.

Heat the oil in a large saucepan over medium heat. Add the onion and cook for 10 minutes, stirring occasionally. Add the ginger, garlic, garam masala, cumin, turmeric, and cayenne and cook for 2 minutes. Add the beans, tomato purée, just-boiled water, fenugreek leaves, butter, ½ teaspoon salt, and a generous grind of black pepper. Stir well, cover, and cook for 10 minutes. Add a splash more water if the beans look dry, then use the back of a wooden spoon to mash a few of the beans into the sauce to thicken it. Taste and adjust the seasoning to your preference. Serve topped with the coriander.

Aubergine and Lentil Tahchin

SERVES 6

AUBERGINE

3 medium aubergines, cut into 2.5cm-thick rounds

Vegetable oil

Salt

RICE

440g white basmati rice

1 teaspoon saffron strands

Pinch sugar

3 tablespoons just-boiled water

Vegetable oil

45g butter

1 medium onion, finely chopped

4 fat garlic cloves, finely grated

1½ teaspoons ground cumin

1½ teaspoons ground coriander

½ teaspoon ground turmeric

½ teaspoon ground cinnamon

½ teaspoon Aleppo pepper or other mild chilli flakes

250g cooked brown or green lentils

2 large eggs plus 2 large egg yolks

250g Greek-style yoghurt

Salt and freshly ground black pepper

TOPPING

30g butter

1½ tablespoons sugar

5 tablespoons barberries

1 tablespoon slivered pistachios

This sunshine-yellow layered Iranian rice cake is a real showstopper when it's brought to the table whole, adorned with its ruby-red glistening fried barberry topping. Traditionally made with poached chicken or lamb, this vegetarian version uses aubergine and lentils and is updated from the recipe in my first book, *The Saffron Tales*, adding lentils for an extra protein hit. There's no getting around the fact that there are a few steps involved, but it can be made in advance and assembled, ready for you to pop into the oven 1½ hours before serving to guests. A can of lentils is one way to speed up the process, but if you'd rather cook them from scratch, simply cook 125g lentils in a pot of boiling water for 15 to 20 minutes, until they are soft (you can do this in advance, or use up any cooked lentils you might have in the fridge). A thick and creamy Spinach Borani (page 123) and a sharp Everyday Middle Eastern Chopped Salad (page 85) are essential accompaniments, so plan on making these all together. You'll need a 2.6 litre baking dish. I tend to use a clear glass Pyrex dish, so I can see how brown the crust of the rice gets and take it out when it's golden. (See the photo on page 182.)

Preheat the oven to 200°C/Fan 180°C/Gas Mark 6.

Arrange the aubergine slices on a large baking sheet, brush with vegetable oil on both sides, and season generously with salt. Transfer to the oven and bake for 20 to 25 minutes, until cooked through. When done, set aside as you prepare the other ingredients.

While the aubergine is cooking, rinse the rice in several changes of cold water until the water runs clear, then leave to soak in a large bowl of water for 15 minutes. Drain.

Fill a large saucepan with water and bring to the boil. Add 2 tablespoons salt and the rice (don't worry, the rice cooks for only a short time in the water, so it won't be salty). Cook for 6 to 7 minutes, until the rice grains are soft on the outside but still firm in the middle. Drain and rinse with cold water to stop the cooking.

Grind the saffron and sugar in a mortar and pestle. Add the just-boiled water and leave to steep for 5 minutes.

Heat 2 tablespoons vegetable oil with 15g of the butter in a large saucepan over medium heat. Add the onion and cook for 10 minutes, until softened. Add the garlic, cumin, coriander, turmeric, cinnamon, chilli flakes, ½ teaspoon salt, and ¼ teaspoon black pepper and cook for 2 minutes. Add the lentils and stir well. Cook for 2 minutes, then remove the pan from the heat.

In a large bowl, beat the eggs and egg yolks, yoghurt, saffron liquid, and 1 teaspoon salt. Gently fold the rice into the mixture until it is evenly coated with the yoghurt mixture.

Rub the remaining 30g butter over the bottom and sides of a 2.6 litre baking dish. Spoon half of the rice into the dish and press it down evenly. Add a layer of aubergine, then a layer of lentils, and finish with a layer of the remaining rice.

Cover the dish tightly with foil and bake for 1¼ to 1½ hours, until the rice at the bottom of the tahchin is crisp and golden brown. Set aside to cool while you make the topping.

Heat the butter in a small saucepan over medium-low heat. Add the sugar and cook, stirring, until the sugar has dissolved. Add the barberries and cook for a minute or two, until they plump up and soften, then add the pistachios and cook for a further minute, stirring often.

To invert the tahchin, place a large serving plate on top of the baking dish and quickly and confidently turn it over. Top with the barberries and pistachios and serve.

Halloumi Lasagne

SERVES 4 TO 6

Lasagne is one of my ultimate comfort foods, and in the case of this particular lasagne, it's not hard to understand why. Soft layers of pasta and béchamel are interspersed with a rich tomato sauce laden with hearty Mediterranean vegetables such as squash, courgette, pepper, and aubergine and then topped with thin slices of halloumi cheese for an irresistible appeal. I serve it with a crisp salad and some garlic bread. This freezes well, so it's great for batch-cooking. **(See the photo on page 186).**

550g peeled and deseeded butternut squash, cut into small pieces
450g courgettes, cut into small pieces
1 red pepper, cut into small pieces
2 medium aubergines, cut into small pieces
Olive oil
1 onion, finely chopped
4 fat garlic cloves, finely grated
500ml passata
1 teaspoon balsamic vinegar
2 teaspoons dried oregano
1 teaspoon sweet paprika
½ teaspoon Aleppo pepper or other mild chilli flakes
¼ teaspoon ground cinnamon
120ml water
12 lasagne sheets
Salt and freshly ground black pepper

BÉCHAMEL SAUCE

75g butter
80g plain flour
700ml milk
¼ teaspoon ground white pepper
Pinch ground nutmeg
50g finely grated Parmesan cheese
Salt

TOPPINGS

200g block halloumi, very thinly sliced
25g finely grated Parmesan cheese

Preheat the oven to 180°C/Fan 160°C/Gas Mark 4.

Combine the squash, courgettes, red pepper, and aubergines on a large baking sheet (use two sheets if needed), drizzle with 3 tablespoons olive oil, season with a generous pinch of salt, and mix well with your hands. Roast for 30 minutes, or until soft.

Heat 2 tablespoons olive oil in a large saucepan over medium heat. Add the onion and cook, stirring, for 12 minutes. Add the garlic and cook for 1 minute. Stir in the passata, vinegar, oregano, paprika, chilli flakes, and cinnamon and cook for 5 minutes, stirring often. Add the roasted vegetables and season with ¾ teaspoon salt and ¼ teaspoon black pepper. Add the water to loosen the mixture and mix well.

To make the béchamel, combine the butter and flour in a small saucepan over low heat, stirring to form a paste. Cook for 3 to 4 minutes, stirring often. Add the milk, white pepper, and nutmeg and whisk for 1 to 2 minutes, until the sauce is thick and smooth. Stir in the 50g Parmesan and ¼ teaspoon salt.

Now begin layering. Spoon one-third of the vegetable mixture into a 2.6 litre glass baking dish and cover with one-third of the lasagne sheets in a single layer. Top with one-third of the béchamel. Repeat with two more layers each of vegetables, pasta, and béchamel. Top the lasagne with the halloumi and the 25g Parmesan.

Cover the dish with foil and bake for 20 minutes. Remove the foil and bake for another 25 minutes, or until the topping is golden brown. Let stand for 10 minutes to allow the filling to settle before cutting the lasagne.

Coconut Chana Daal

SERVES 4

400g chana daal, rinsed
1.2 litres just-boiled water
1½ teaspoons garam masala
1 teaspoon ground turmeric
1 teaspoon ground coriander
250ml full-fat coconut milk
Salt

TARKA

1 tablespoon vegetable oil, or 15g butter or ghee
Seeds from 3 green cardamom pods, lightly crushed
1¼ teaspoons cumin seeds
1 teaspoon yellow or brown mustard seeds
10 dried curry leaves
2 red chillis, halved and deseeded

This luscious, creamy, coconut-infused daal is made with yellow split peas, also known as chana daal, and infused with the cardamom-and curry leaf-spiced tarka. The cooking time will vary depending on the age of your split peas, so the timings given here are approximate. I don't quite know why, but I've been told that split peas that are glossy take longer to cook than the ones that look dull in colour, so if you have the option of choosing which ones you buy, have a look at the packet and get the latter. I love serving this with the Punjabi Spiced Vegetable Medley (page 111) and a side of rice, flatbreads, and mango or lime achaar (South Asian spicy pickle), as pictured.

Rinse the split peas and let soak in a large bowl of cold water for at least 6 hours, or overnight.

Drain the split peas, transfer to a saucepan, and top with the just-boiled water. Bring to a rolling boil over high heat and boil for 5 minutes, using a spoon to remove any scum that rises to the surface. Add the garam masala, turmeric, and coriander and stir well, then cover, turn the heat down to medium, and cook for 45 minutes.

Add the coconut milk and 1 teaspoon salt, turn the heat up to medium-high, and cook until the lentils are beginning to break down and meld into each other, 30 to 60 minutes. When they are completely soft and creamy, you know the daal is ready.

To make the tarka, heat the oil in a small pan over medium heat. Add the cardamom seeds, cumin seeds, mustard seeds, curry leaves, and chillis and stir briskly for 1 to 2 minutes to toast the spices (be careful, as they might pop and splutter!). Stir the tarka into the daal and serve.

Tofu and Sweet Potato Massaman Curry

SERVES 4

300g firm tofu
3 tablespoons cornflour or plain flour
Vegetable oil
1 shallot, thinly sliced
2 garlic cloves, finely grated
1½ tablespoons finely grated ginger
3 tablespoons massaman or red curry paste
1 (400ml) tin full-fat coconut milk
250ml vegetable stock
3 tablespoons crunchy peanut butter
1 tablespoon lime juice, or more to taste
1 tablespoon soft light brown sugar
400g sweet potatoes, peeled and cut into small pieces
400g potatoes, peeled and cut into small pieces
100g green beans, cut into rough 5cm pieces
35g roasted peanuts, chopped
Soy sauce, tamari, or vegan or traditional fish sauce, to taste (optional)
Sliced red chillis, to taste (optional)

It's hard to pick a favourite Thai curry, but if I had to it would be massaman. It's comfort food in a bowl for me, no doubt aided by its winning double-carb combination of rice with potatoes and the interplay of creamy coconut milk and crunchy peanuts that I find utterly moreish. Massaman curry is traditionally made with beef or chicken, but in this version I use tofu, which soaks up the aromatic sauce wonderfully. I've suggested a tip for pressing tofu, which is how I usually prepare it at home to improve the texture, but it isn't essential if you don't have time. If you are making this for vegetarians, you may want to check that your curry paste doesn't include crustaceans. Serve with white rice.

Spread a tea towel over a plate. Place the tofu on the tea towel, cover with another tea towel, and place a large plate with a couple of tins (such as beans or tomatoes) on top. Leave the tofu to gently drain off its excess water for about 15 minutes. Remove the tofu from the tea towels and cut it into small rectangular pieces, about 4 × 1.25cm. Toss with the cornflour.

Heat 2 tablespoons oil in a large saucepan over medium heat. Add the tofu and cook for 2 to 3 minutes on each side, until crisp and browned. You might need to do this in batches, adding a little more oil as you go along. Transfer to a plate lined with kitchen paper to drain.

Wipe the pan clean and heat 2 tablespoons oil over medium heat. Add the shallot and cook for 2 minutes, or until soft. Add the garlic and ginger and cook for 1 minute. Add the curry paste and cook, stirring often, for 1 minute. Add the coconut milk, stock, peanut butter, lime juice, and sugar and gently stir or whisk until the peanut butter has melted. Stir in the sweet potatoes, potatoes, and green beans. Cover and cook for 15 minutes, or until the potatoes are soft. Add the tofu, peanuts, a dash of soy sauce (if using), and sliced chillis (if using). Taste and adjust the seasoning – you might want more lime juice.

Thai Fried Rice

SERVES 4

Fried rice is what I make when I want to use up any vegetables that are getting past their prime. I like to cook it Thai style, with plenty of garlic and chillis, using nutty brown rice for extra texture and flavour. Fried rice is best made with day-old rice, but you can make it with fresh rice too; just let it drain and dry well first. Traditionally fish sauce, oyster sauce, and the Thai seasoning Golden Mountain flavour this, but when cooking for vegetarians I substitute vegan "fish" sauce and mushroom-based vegan "oyster" sauce, both of which are readily available in health food shops and online. Fish sauce and oyster sauces can vary significantly in salt and sugar levels, so add more if you feel your rice needs it – remember that you can always add but you can't take away! I like to keep the heat levels of the chilli mild and suggest guests add prik nam pla and fresh lime to their own portions as desired.

PRIK NAM PLA

- 1 to 2 tablespoons chopped red chillis
- 60ml vegan or traditional fish sauce
- 1 tablespoon lime juice
- 1 garlic clove, finely grated or thinly sliced (optional)
- ½ teaspoon sugar

- Vegetable oil
- 1 or 2 shallots, thinly sliced
- 4 garlic cloves, finely chopped
- 2 or 3 red or green chillis, finely chopped
- 1 large carrot, chopped
- 100g tenderstem broccoli or gai lan, chopped
- 5 baby corn, chopped
- 2 tablespoons vegan or traditional oyster sauce
- 1 tablespoon vegan or traditional fish sauce
- 200g cooked brown rice
- 2 spring onions, finely chopped
- 2 limes
- 1 large handful Thai basil leaves
- 4 large eggs

To make the prik nam pla, mix the chillis, fish sauce, lime juice, garlic, if using, and sugar together in a small bowl. Set aside.

Heat 2 tablespoons oil in a wok or large frying pan over medium heat. Add the shallots and cook for 3 to 4 minutes, until they have softened, then add the garlic and chillis and cook for 30 seconds. Add the carrot, tenderstem broccoli, and corn and cook for 3 minutes. Add the oyster sauce and fish sauce and mix well. Add the rice and spring onions and cook for 4 minutes, mixing until well combined. Squeeze over the juice of half a lime and stir in the basil. Mix again and remove the pan from the heat.

Heat 2 tablespoons oil in another frying pan over medium heat. Crack the eggs into the pan and fry until cooked through. (My tip is to tilt the pan with one hand and use the oil that falls into a corner to spoon over the yolk to slightly cook it). Transfer to a plate lined with kitchen paper to soak up any excess oil.

To serve, spoon some rice onto each plate, top with a fried egg, and serve with small bowls of prik nam pla and lime wedges.

Pasta with Aubergine, Tomatoes, and Capers

SERVES 4

2 large aubergines
Olive oil
4 garlic cloves, thinly sliced
2 (400g) tins chopped tomatoes
1 teaspoon sugar
1 teaspoon dried oregano
½ teaspoon Aleppo pepper or other mild chilli flakes
400g spaghetti
2 tablespoons capers, drained and rinsed
Extra-virgin olive oil
1 handful basil leaves
Grated Parmesan cheese or pangrattato (page 161), for topping
Salt and freshly ground black pepper

The island of Sicily has an enviable cuisine, borne from the melding of influences that have gathered there over several millennia due to its position as a crossroads between Europe and North Africa. Pasta alla Norma, the Italian name for this famous Sicilian dish, is rich with the sweetness of aubergine. Serve with a green salad and a smattering of Parmesan or pangrattato – crispy, garlicky, fried breadcrumbs.

Preheat the oven to 180°C/Fan 160°C/Gas Mark 4. Line two large baking sheets with foil or baking paper.

Use a small paring knife or vegetable peeler to shave strips of the aubergine skin, until they look stripey. Cut the aubergine into 2.5cm chunks and spread out on the prepared baking sheets. Toss with 3 tablespoons olive oil and sprinkle with ½ teaspoon salt. Roast for 25 to 30 minutes, until cooked through.

While the aubergine is roasting, heat 2 tablespoons olive oil in a large saucepan over medium-low heat. Add the garlic and cook for 2 minutes. Add the tomatoes, sugar, oregano, chilli flakes, ½ teaspoon salt, and ¼ teaspoon black pepper. Cover and cook for 30 minutes.

Meanwhile, cook the pasta in a large pot of well-salted water according to the package instructions until al dente. Drain, reserving 60ml of the cooking water.

Stir the aubergine, capers, and 2 tablespoons extra-virgin olive oil into the tomato sauce, adding some of the reserved pasta water if the sauce looks dry. Cook for 3 minutes, then taste and adjust the seasoning. Remove the pan from the heat and stir in the basil.

Add the cooked pasta to the tomato sauce and mix well, being careful not to break up the aubergine. Top with Parmesan or pangrattato and more black pepper.

Lentil and Mushroom Ragù

SERVES 6

150g green or brown lentils
Vegetable oil
1 medium onion, chopped
4 garlic cloves, crushed
1½ teaspoons ground cumin
2 (400g) tins chopped tomatoes
350g chestnut mushrooms, roughly chopped
250ml just-boiled water
2 teaspoons dried oregano
½ teaspoon ground cinnamon
½ teaspoon Aleppo pepper or other mild chilli flakes
1 teaspoon sugar
2 bay leaves
1 tablespoon Worcestershire sauce
2 teaspoons soy sauce or tamari
Extra-virgin olive oil
Salt and freshly ground black pepper

The Brit in me loves a good "spag bol", which was probably the first meal I taught myself how to cook when I was a teenager. Meat-free versions of it can be just as comforting and homey, and this mushroom and lentil ragù is what I cook when I need something hearty to warm me up from the inside. My ingredient list reflects what I most commonly cook with, taking influence from the Mediterranean with the hints of cinnamon, cumin, and oregano, and from the UK, with its addition of Worcestershire sauce, and a dash of East Asian soy sauce for an umami hit. Serve with any pasta – I love it with ribbons of tagliatelle – or stuffed into a baked potato, with generous shavings of Cheddar or Parmesan on top.

Rinse the lentils and transfer to a small saucepan. Cover with just-boiled water and cook over medium heat for 15 to 20 minutes, until the lentils are completely soft but still have some shape. Drain and set aside.

While the lentils are cooking, heat 2 tablespoons vegetable oil in a large saucepan over medium heat. Add the onion and cook for 15 minutes, stirring occasionally, until soft. Add the garlic and cumin and cook for 2 minutes. Add the tomatoes, mushrooms, just-boiled water, oregano, cinnamon, chilli flakes, sugar, bay leaves, 1 teaspoon salt, and a generous grind of black pepper and stir well. Cover, turn the heat down to medium-low, and cook for 25 minutes, stirring occasionally.

Add the lentils, Worcestershire sauce, soy sauce, 4 tablespoons extra-virgin olive oil, and another generous grind of black pepper to the tomato sauce. Cook for 5 minutes for the flavours to come together, then taste and adjust the seasoning. Serve drizzled with more extra-virgin olive oil.

Lemony Chickpeas
with Asparagus and Kale

SERVES 2 TO 3 AS A MAIN WITH BREAD

- 2 tablespoons vegetable oil
- 1 medium onion, chopped
- 3 fat garlic cloves, finely grated
- 1 (400g) tin chickpeas, drained and rinsed
- 250ml vegetable stock
- 140g kale, shredded
- 100g asparagus, cut into 4cm pieces
- 1½ teaspoons grated lemon zest
- 1½ tablespoons lemon juice, or more to taste
- Extra-virgin olive oil
- Aleppo pepper or other mild chilli flakes, for garnish
- Salt and freshly ground black pepper

This simple and light spring dish is easy to prepare and offers the flexibility of being able to serve in several ways. I've eaten these chickpeas stirred into pasta, spooned over rice, or squashed onto toast with hummus and then topped with thin slices of sweet tomatoes. As always, be generous with the good-quality extra-virgin olive oil, as this dish can take a lot!

Heat the vegetable oil in a large sauté pan over medium heat. Add the onion and ¼ teaspoon salt and cook, stirring occasionally, for 12 minutes, or until softened. Add the garlic and cook for 2 minutes. Add the chickpeas and stock, stir everything together, and cook until bubbling. Add the kale, cover, and cook for 8 to 10 minutes, stirring occasionally, until it has softened.

Then add the asparagus, lemon zest and juice, a generous grind of black pepper, and 2 tablespoons extra-virgin olive oil and cook for a further 3 minutes or so, until the asparagus has just cooked through. Taste and adjust the seasoning; you may want a bit more salt or lemon.

Serve in shallow bowls, sprinkled generously with chilli flakes. I can never resist more olive oil at this stage, so this is the point I would judiciously add a drizzle to my serving. You do you, though.

Dreamy Desserts

Life is uncertain. Eat dessert first.
– **ERNESTINE ULMER**

For many years I had a wicked sweet tooth, and my early forays into the kitchen focussed on baking pies, tarts, cakes, and cookies, which I served to appreciative housemates in numerous flat shares. My sweet tooth has waned since, and only a special dessert has me reaching for second helpings. Yet for the recipes in this chapter, I reached for thirds! The desserts here fall into two categories: those with sharp, fruity flavours and those filled with heady, warming spices. You'll find a maple and clove-spiked carrot cake, a rhubarb and cardamom tart, a saffron and rose water-infused rice pudding, and many others. Even if you don't consider yourself a dessert person, I hope these recipes remind you that we all deserve a little sweetness in life.

Rhubarb and Cardamom Tart

SERVES 8

PASTRY

150g plain flour, sifted
25g icing sugar
80g unsalted butter, cut into small cubes
1 large egg yolk
2 to 3 tablespoons cold water
Salt

FRUIT

300g rhubarb, cut into 5cm pieces
2 tablespoons caster sugar

FILLING

170g unsalted butter
170g caster sugar
2 large eggs
170g ground almonds
1 tablespoon grated orange zest
1 teaspoon vanilla extract
Seeds from 10 cardamom pods, ground or a scant ½ teaspoon ground cardamom
Salt

There is something intrinsically cheerful about rhubarb, with its gloriously tart, vivid pink stalks. Here I've paired them with a cardamom and orange-infused almond frangipane encased in a buttery crust, making a dessert that is soft, crunchy, sweet, and sour all at once. You can serve this warm, with the filling unset and almost pudding-like, alongside a dollop of crème fraîche, or at room temperature once it's been left to cool for a few hours. I find it helpful to have baking beans on hand to blind-bake the tart crust. These are ceramic or metal "beans" that weigh down the base of pastry while it cooks so it doesn't puff up. You can also just use regular dried beans, laid over some foil on top of the pastry. (You can then store these in a jar and reuse for future bakes.) The tart keeps well in an airtight container for up to 2 days. (See the photo on page 203.)

To make the pastry, combine the flour, icing sugar, and ¼ teaspoon salt in a large bowl and use your hands to rub the butter into it until you have a texture resembling breadcrumbs. (Alternatively, you can use a stand mixer fitted with the paddle attachment and mix on low speed.)

Add the egg yolk and then slowly beat in the cold water, 1 tablespoon at a time, until you have a smooth dough. You might not need all the water, so do this in stages. The key is not to overwork the dough or it will end up chewy and elastic instead of crumbly and short.

Mould the dough into a ball and roll it out until it is 3mm thick. Grease a 23cm fluted tart pan and lay the pastry into it, gently pushing into the corners. To avoid shrinkage when it bakes, leave about 2cm pastry hanging over the rim of the tart tin and pinch it lightly to grip the edges. Don't worry about it looking unsightly at this stage; you can trim it after baking if you need to, using a sharp knife. Cover with cling film and refrigerate for at least 1 hour, or up to overnight.

While the dough is chilling, put the chopped rhubarb in a large bowl and sprinkle with the caster sugar. Mix well and leave to macerate for 45 minutes to draw some of the water out of it.

Preheat the oven to 200°C/Fan 180°C/Gas Mark 6.

Prick the base of the pastry a few times with a fork, line with baking paper, and fill with baking beans. Bake for 15 minutes. Remove the paper and weights. Bake for another 5 to 10 minutes, until the pastry is light golden brown. Remove from the oven and let the pastry cool completely while you make the filling.

In an electric mixer, beat the butter and caster sugar together until light and creamy (or use a wooden spoon and a large bowl; it will take more time). Gently beat in the eggs, then fold in the ground almonds, orange zest, vanilla, cardamom, and ¼ teaspoon salt. Spoon the filling into the tart shell and use the back of the spoon to even out the top.

Drain the rhubarb and press the pieces of fruit into the top of the tart. Don't worry if the filling spills over onto the fruit. Bake for 40 minutes, or until the frangipane is set and golden brown on top.

Serve the tart slightly warm, or leave it to firm up and cool for a couple of hours before slicing it.

Quince Crumble

SERVES 4

3 medium quinces (about 850g), peeled, cored, and cut into small chunks
350ml water
3 tablespoons caster sugar
¼ teaspoon ground cloves (about 10 cloves)
½ teaspoon ground cinnamon
Pinch ground nutmeg

CRUMBLE TOPPING
200g plain flour
140g fridge-cold unsalted butter
115g caster sugar
Salt

OPTIONAL TOPPINGS
Custard (recipe follows), ice cream, or double cream

My grandparents' farm in northern Iran had several quince trees, and each year we'd harvest the ambrosial yellow fruits to make sweet and lightly spiced preserves and jams. I've blended those flavours into a classic British fruit crumble, which I have on regular rotation in the colder winter months, as they are quick to make and always comfort. As for what to serve a crumble with – ice cream, double cream, or custard – I let guests decide, but for me, it's always got to be proper, thick, vanilla-infused British custard (which is much more robust than the delicate crème anglaise). I've included a recipe for it on the next page, but ready-made and out of a packet is fine, and what I grew up on, as the whole point of a crumble in my mind is that it should be fuss-free and quick. You can track down quinces in Middle Eastern supermarkets or at farmers' markets, and I occasionally see them in larger supermarkets too. You can also substitute apples. (See the photo on page 206.)

Preheat the oven to 200°C/Fan 180°C/Gas Mark 6.

Combine the quinces, water, sugar, cloves, cinnamon, and nutmeg in a large sauté pan; the fruit should be submerged in the water. Cover and cook over medium heat for 15 minutes, or until soft. Using a slotted spoon, transfer the cooked fruit to a 23cm-deep pie tin or ovenproof dish. Turn the heat up to high and cook the poaching liquid for about 5 minutes, or until it has reduced by half. Pour this liquid over the fruit.

To make the crumble topping, combine the flour, butter, sugar, and ¼ teaspoon salt in a large bowl and mix with your fingers until it resembles breadcrumbs. (You can also pulse it in a food processor.) Spoon the crumble topping over the quinces, lightly pressing down to cover the fruit.

Bake for 40 minutes, or until the crumble is golden brown on top and you can see the fruit bubbling underneath. Spoon into serving bowls and top with the custard, ice cream, or double cream.

Custard

500ml whole milk
½ teaspoon vanilla extract
3 large egg yolks
1½ tablespoons plain flour
2 tablespoons caster sugar

Warm the milk and vanilla in a small saucepan over medium heat. When it starts to bubble, remove the pan from heat. In a large bowl, whisk together the egg yolks, flour, and sugar. Gently pour the warmed milk into the eggs, one ladleful at a time, stirring while you do so. Return the mixture to the pan, turn the heat down to low, and cook for 10 minutes, or until the custard has thickened, gently whisking the whole time so it doesn't stick to the bottom of the pan. Serve warm, spooned over servings of the crumble.

Dark Chocolate and Dried Lime Tart

SERVES 8

Many years ago, I visited an artisan chocolate store in northern Tehran where Persian flavours were delicately blended with milk and dark chocolates, resulting in some magnificent combinations. This tart takes inspiration from some truffles I sampled that day and brings together the wicked bitterness of dark chocolate with the bright citrus of dried limes. It's intense, so you need only a sliver to be satisfied, making it perfect after a meal, served with black tea or coffee. Any leftovers can be stored in the fridge for up to 2 days.

BASE

200g digestive biscuits
115g unsalted butter, melted

FILLING

4 dried limes
350ml double cream
85g caster sugar
370g dark chocolate (70%), broken into pieces
½ teaspoon vanilla extract
1 tablespoon pistachios, for garnish
Dried edible rose petals, for garnish
Salt

Blitz the digestive biscuits in a food processor until they have the consistency of breadcrumbs. Transfer to a bowl and stir in the melted butter until the mixture starts to come together. Spoon this into a 20cm tart tin with a removable bottom and press into an even layer. Transfer to the fridge to chill and set while you make the filling.

Put the dried limes in a small bag and crack them by hitting them with a rolling pin a few times until they break into small shards. Transfer to a small saucepan and add the cream and sugar. Let infuse over low heat for 10 minutes, stirring occasionally. Remove from the heat and leave to cool for 5 minutes.

To make the filling, melt the chocolate in the microwave or by placing it in a heatproof bowl set over a saucepan of simmering water. Strain the lime-infused cream through a fine-mesh sieve into the chocolate and press against the pieces of dried lime with a wooden spoon to extract all their flavour. Add the vanilla and a pinch of salt and whisk until you have thick and glossy filling.

Remove the base from the fridge and spoon the chocolate ganache into it. Return it to the fridge and chill for at least 1 hour. Smash the pistachios with a mortar and pestle and sprinkle over the tart along with rose petals before serving.

Pumpkin, Pecan, and Brown Butter Blondies

MAKES 12 BLONDIES

- 225g unsalted butter, cut into small cubes
- 85g pecans, roughly chopped
- 225g plain flour
- ½ teaspoon baking powder
- 1 teaspoon ground cinnamon
- ⅛ teaspoon ground cloves
- ⅛ teaspoon ground nutmeg
- 115g caster sugar
- 115g soft dark brown sugar
- 2 large eggs, beaten
- 230g pumpkin purée
- 2 teaspoons vanilla extract
- Salt

This is everything I love in a baked treat: sweet, sticky, salty, and spiced. Browning butter is a very simple technique but does involve a little attention, as you have to watch the melted butter closely so it doesn't burn. It gives these blondies a magnificent butterscotch flavour. Blondies should be fudgy and dense in the middle, so take them out of the oven when they are ever so slightly undercooked; they will cook more as they are cooling in the tin. As ovens can vary, check after 16 minutes of baking by inserting a cocktail stick or the tip of a sharp knife into the middle of the tray. It should come away a little bit sticky but mostly dry. If it's completely dry, then you've gone too far with the baking (though they will still taste wonderful).

Preheat the oven to 180°C/Fan 160°C/Gas Mark 4. Grease a 23 × 33cm baking tin and line with baking paper.

Put the butter in a small saucepan set over medium heat, stirring gently as it melts and then comes to a simmer. Keep observing the melted butter as it bubbles away. First it will froth and then, over the course of a few minutes, its colour will darken to a light brown and it will take on a slightly nutty aroma. Depending on the size of your pan, this can take anywhere from 3 to 6 minutes. As soon as you see some light brown specks form at the bottom of the pan, mix well and then pour the butter into a bowl to cool.

Add the pecans to the now-empty saucepan and toast over medium heat for 2 minutes, then transfer them to a separate bowl to cool.

Sift the flour, ¾ teaspoon salt, baking powder, cinnamon, cloves, and nutmeg into a large bowl. Add the sugars, beaten eggs, cooled brown butter, pumpkin purée, and vanilla. Fold

continues ►

together just until there are no more streaks of flour and then stop. (If you overmix, the blondies can take on more of a cake consistency, but again it's not the end of the world and they will still be delicious!)

Spoon the batter into the prepared baking tin and bake for 16 to 18 minutes, until the top is set and a cocktail stick comes out with a few crumbs but isn't completely sticky. Leave to cool before slicing.

Poached Pears
with Cinnamon Cream

SERVES 4

1 (750ml) bottle red wine
200g granulated sugar
1 cinnamon stick
Seeds of 1 vanilla pod
4 large pears, peeled

CINNAMON CREAM
300ml double cream
4 tablespoons icing sugar
1 teaspoon grated lemon zest
¼ teaspoon ground cinnamon

Pears are a great carrier for cinnamon, and in this recipe you get a double hit in the poaching liquid and the whipped cream. Just be sure to choose firm pears, as you don't want them to turn too mushy when they cook. If you or your eating companions don't drink alcohol, you can use non-alcoholic red wine, which is becoming more widely available and works just as well.

In a large saucepan, combine the wine, granulated sugar, cinnamon stick, and vanilla seeds. Bring to the boil over medium heat, stirring occasionally to dissolve the sugar.

Add the pears and pour in enough water to cover. Turn the heat down to medium-low and poach the pears for 45 minutes, or until tender but not mushy. Transfer the pears to a bowl. Turn up the heat and bring the poaching liquid to a rolling boil; cook until reduced by half, about 10 minutes. Remove the pan from the heat and set aside to cool. If you aren't eating the pears right away, pop them back into the poaching liquid to continue to infuse with the flavours.

When ready to serve, make the cinnamon cream. With an electric mixer, whip the cream, icing sugar, lemon zest, and ground cinnamon until soft peaks form.

To serve, plate the pears and spoon over some of the poaching liquid and a good dollop of cinnamon cream.

Saffron Rice Pudding (Sholeh Zard)

SERVES 6

200g short-grain white rice
1.2 litres plus 2 tablespoons just-boiled water
150g plus a pinch granulated sugar
½ teaspoon saffron strands
Seeds from 4 cardamom pods, ground
1 tablespoon rose water
30g unsalted butter
Ground cinnamon, to decorate
2 tablespoons crushed pistachios

This traditional Iranian pudding has a sunshine-yellow glow from saffron and pairs the classic Persian combination of cardamom and rose water for an extremely aromatic dessert. Sholeh zard is often made for Islamic holy months in Iran, such as Ramadan or Muharram, and for commemorative events such as the anniversary of someone passing. It's too good not to enjoy year-round, though, and is an easy dessert to make ahead when you are entertaining. For best results, cook the rice until completely soft – much more than if you were making a Western-style rice pudding. You can serve it either from one large dish or in small glasses or bowls. It keeps well in the fridge for up to 3 days.

Combine the rice and 1.2 litres of the just-boiled water in a large saucepan. Cover and cook over medium heat for 40 minutes, stirring occasionally, or until completely soft.

Meanwhile, grind the saffron and a pinch of sugar in a mortar and pestle. Add the remaining 2 tablespoons just-boiled water and leave to steep for 5 minutes.

When the rice is ready, stir in the remaining 150g sugar, saffron mixture, cardamom, and rose water and cook for 5 minutes. Remove the pan from the heat and stir in the butter.

Transfer to a serving bowl or to individual serving glasses. Decorate with the cinnamon – I like to make a cross in small dishes or run it around the edges of a large dish – and the crushed pistachios. Leave to cool completely before serving.

Spiced Carrot Cake
with Maple Cream Cheese Frosting

SERVES 8

200ml vegetable oil
285g soft dark brown sugar
4 large eggs
Grated zest and juice of 1 orange
250g plain flour
1 teaspoon baking powder
½ teaspoon bicarbonate of soda
¾ teaspoon ground cinnamon
¼ teaspoon ground cloves
½ teaspoon ground ginger
250g grated carrots
100g walnuts, chopped
Salt

ICING
115g salted butter, softened
130g icing sugar
3 tablespoons maple syrup
1 teaspoon grated orange zest
1 tablespoon orange juice
Pinch ground cloves
250g full-fat cream cheese

This cake is one to make when you want to warm hearts: a thick, dense, and moist carrot cake, spiced with cloves, ginger, and cinnamon and topped with a tangy orange cream cheese frosting. Using oil instead of butter results in a lighter texture and softer crumb, and the brown sugar imparts a deliciously wicked caramel flavour. If you want to make it in advance it will keep well in an airtight container for up to 2 days, but it's best to eat it on the day that you ice it.

Preheat the oven to 180°C/Fan 160°C/Gas Mark 4. Grease two 20cm round cake tins and line with baking paper.

Lightly beat the oil, brown sugar, eggs, and orange zest and juice in a large bowl. Sift in the flour, baking powder, bicarbonate of soda, cinnamon, cloves, ginger, and ¼ teaspoon salt. Fold in the carrots and most of the nuts, reserving a few for garnish.

Pour the batter into the prepared cake tins and bake for 30 minutes, or until a skewer inserted into the middle comes out clean. Leave the cakes to cool in the tins for 5 minutes, then turn out onto a cooling rack to cool completely.

To make the icing, beat the butter, icing sugar, maple syrup, orange zest and juice, cloves, and cream cheese with an electric mixer until pale and smooth. Pop the icing in the fridge to chill and thicken for at least 30 minutes.

Once the cake has cooled, spread with the icing, using it to sandwich the two layers together and ice its top. Add the reserved nuts to decorate.

Apricot, Pistachio, and Tahini Granola Bars

MAKES 6 TO 8 BARS

175g jumbo rolled oats
125g dried apricots, roughly chopped
50g pistachios
1 tablespoon pumpkin seeds
1 tablespoon sunflower seeds
1 tablespoon sesame seeds
1 tablespoon milled flax seeds
1 teaspoon ground cinnamon
75g coconut oil or butter
65g soft dark brown sugar
60g tahini
3 tablespoons honey or maple syrup
1 ripe banana, mashed
1 teaspoon vanilla extract
Salt

I am obsessed with these sweet treats. Soft, sticky, packed with nuts and seeds, and sweetened with banana and honey, these irresistible granola bars are perfect for when you are craving something sweet but still relatively healthy. They also work well as a light breakfast, with a mug of hot tea or coffee. The bars keep well in an airtight container for about 3 days and tend to get softer and chewier after 24 hours, so they are great to make ahead. I use a 16cm-square baking tin for this.

Preheat the oven to 180°C/Fan 160°C/Gas Mark 4. Line a small baking tin with baking paper.

Mix the oats, apricots, pistachios, pumpkin seeds, sunflower seeds, sesame seeds, flax seeds, cinnamon, and ¼ teaspoon salt in a large bowl.

Melt the coconut oil in a small saucepan over low heat. Stir in the brown sugar until melted. Remove from the heat and stir in the tahini, honey, mashed banana, and vanilla. Mix the warm ingredients into the dry ingredients until combined.

Press the oat mixture into the prepared baking tin. Bake for 30 to 35 minutes, until golden brown. Leave to cool before slicing into bars.

Chocolate and Sour Cherry Brownies

MAKES 9 BROWNIES

2 tablespoons milled flax seeds
100ml water
200g dark chocolate (70%), broken into pieces
1 teaspoon vanilla extract
130g plain flour
75g ground almonds
225g caster sugar
2 tablespoons cocoa powder
½ teaspoon baking powder
80ml vegetable oil
80ml cup plant-based milk
55g chopped dried cherries
Salt

This quick and easy chocolate traybake will satisfy any sweet tooth – and it just happens to be vegan! As oven times can vary, keep an eye on the brownies after 22 minutes in; the top should be crisp, but a cocktail stick inserted in the centre should come up still moist with crumbs attached. If it's too gooey, leave it a few minutes longer, though it's worth noting that it will continue cooking a little in the tin. I use oat milk for this recipe.

Preheat the oven to 150°C/Fan 130°C/Gas Mark 2. Grease a 20cm-square baking tin and line with baking paper.

Mix the flax seeds and water in a small bowl and set aside for 5 minutes for it to firm up into a gel-like consistency.

Melt the chocolate in the microwave or by placing it in a heatproof bowl set over a saucepan of simmering water. Remove from the heat and stir in the vanilla.

Combine the flour, ground almonds, sugar, cocoa powder, baking powder, and ½ teaspoon salt in a large bowl. Add the oil, flax seed mixture, melted chocolate, and milk and stir until well combined. Fold in the cherries.

Spoon the batter into the prepared tin. It will be very sticky, so use the back of a spoon to smooth it out. Bake for 25 to 30 minutes, or until the brownies are cooked but a little squidgy in the middle. Leave to cool in the tin before slicing into squares.

Mango, Passion Fruit, and Strawberry Pavlova

SERVES 8

Colourful, sharp fruit; crunchy, chewy meringues; soft, pillowy whipped cream – what's not to love about this dessert? Pavlovas are my go-to when I have people round for dinner as they are so quick to make, and I find that a light and fruity pudding ends a meal in a way that is less likely to induce a food coma but instead keep the evening flowing. Here I pair mangoes, strawberries, and passion fruit for a colourful and tangy topping, but you can substitute any of your favourite fruits when in season.

MERINGUE

- 4 medium egg whites
- 215g caster sugar
- 1 teaspoon white wine vinegar
- 1 teaspoon vanilla extract
- 1 teaspoon cornflour
- Salt

FILLING

- 350ml double cream
- 1 teaspoon icing sugar

TOPPINGS

- 170g diced mango
- Seeds from 5 passion fruit
- 1 large handful fresh strawberries, sliced

Preheat the oven to 150°C/Fan 130°C/Gas Mark 2. Line a large baking sheet with baking paper.

In a large bowl, whisk the egg whites until they form stiff peaks, then whisk in the caster sugar, a little at a time, until the meringue looks glossy. Whisk in the vinegar, vanilla, cornflour, and a pinch of salt.

Spread the meringue on the prepared baking sheet into a disc about 23cm across, creating a small crater by making the sides slightly higher than the middle.

Transfer to the oven and turn the heat down to 130°C/Fan 120°C/Gas Mark 1. Bake for 1 hour, or until it is puffed up and hardened on the outside. Turn off the oven and let the meringue cool completely inside the oven.

With an electric hand mixer, whip the cream and icing sugar until you get soft peaks. Spread the filling over the top of the meringue, then top with the mango, passion fruit, and strawberries. Serve immediately.

Mango Sticky Rice

SERVES 4

250g Thai sticky rice
1 (400ml) tin full-fat coconut milk
50g granulated sugar
2 ripe mangoes, peeled, pitted, and sliced
White or black sesame seeds, toasted
Salt

The winning combination of sticky rice and coconut milk, served with sweet and juicy mangoes, transports me to the bustling streets of Bangkok, where I always buy this Thai dessert from street vendors to eat for my breakfast. My version uses a few shortcuts to save on cooking time, as traditional sticky rice can take quite a while to prepare. To cook it, I use a simple bamboo steamer over a saucepan, but you can use any kind of steamer that you have on hand. Just be sure to line the base so the rice doesn't stick.

Put the rice in a large bowl, cover with cold water, and leave to soak for 4 hours.

Pour about 10cm of just-boiled water into a large saucepan. Line a steamer with steamer liners or pierced baking paper. Drain the rice and transfer to the steamer, then place it on top of the pan. Cover and steam over medium-low heat for 30 to 35 minutes, until the rice is cooked – it should look translucent and glossy.

Heat the coconut milk, sugar, and 1 teaspoon salt in a small saucepan over medium heat, stirring frequently. When the milk is hot and the sugar has dissolved, remove the pan from the heat.

Mix 250ml of the hot coconut milk into the cooked rice and stir well. (It's important to do this mixing of the coconut milk and rice when they are both still hot, as that enables the rice to absorb the liquid better.) Cover and leave to stand for 15 minutes.

Use a small bowl to form rounds of rice and invert onto serving plates. Add mango to each and spoon over the remaining coconut milk. Garnish with the sesame seeds.

Mr.MOMO
MANGOES

Baked Stuffed Apples

SERVES 6

6 apples
45g soft light brown sugar
50g unsalted mixed nuts (I use a mixture of walnuts and pistachios)
6 dried apricots
¾ teaspoon ground cinnamon
¼ teaspoon ground allspice
55g butter, cut into small pieces and softened, plus more if needed
120ml just-boiled water

Comfort Me with Apples **is the title of a memoir by celebrated food writer, editor, and restaurant critic Ruth Reichl that started me on the path to writing my first book. I found an old copy on a bookshelf in a rustic bungalow where I was staying in Thailand and was swept away for the next few days, immersed in her evocative writing. It showed me how food could tell the most powerful and personal of stories and inspired me to tell some stories of my own in** ***The Saffron Tales*****. This is a recipe that represents how I cook with apples for comfort and involves baking them with brown sugar and butter. The best apples for this recipe can hold up under the heat and won't collapse when cooked, such as Pink Lady or Gala. As apple sizes can vary considerably, use the stuffing as an approximation and add more if you need to. I like to serve these warm, with a dollop of crème fraîche or strained Greek-style yoghurt and a drizzle of honey.**

Preheat the oven to 180°C/Fan 160°C/Gas Mark 4.

Place one apple on a cutting board and use a small paring knife to carefully cut around the stem at its top and base. Carefully cut away the inner core, creating a hole about 2.5cm wide (you don't need to be exact; this will depend on the size of the apple and the size of the core). Repeat for the remaining apples.

Combine the brown sugar, nuts, apricots, cinnamon, and allspice in a food processor and blitz until ground and the mixture comes together. Divide the filling into six equal portions. Roll each portion into a sausage shape and push into each apple. Place a small knob of butter on top of each apple and rub the remaining butter all over the apples (if your apples are on the larger size, use a bit more butter). Place the apples in a 23 × 33cm baking dish and pour in the just-boiled water. Bake until soft and golden, 25 to 30 minutes.

Plate the apples and spoon over any sticky juices. If any of the stuffing has fallen out, sprinkle it on top of the apples.

Toward a Fairer Food System

IN RECENT YEARS, more and more people are choosing to incorporate more vegetables into their diet for a variety of health, ethical, socioeconomic, and environmental reasons. It's not hard to understand why.

The global food system and modern ways in which we produce food involve aggressive industrial farming practices that are harmful for animal welfare, destructive to soil and biodiversity, instrumental in producing dangerous climate emissions, and often implicated in serious workers' rights abuses (predominantly against migrants, and almost exclusively against people of colour). Ours is a highly inefficient system characterised by striking inequalities.

According to the United Nations, we have the capacity to produce enough food to feed the world – yet much of this food is badly distributed and unhealthy, and the way it is grown and transported is toxic for the planet. According to the World Food Programme, around one-third of the food produced globally is lost or wasted in the supply chain. In the United States alone, according to the Environmental Protection Agency, over 66 billion tons of food is wasted each year, amounting to around 40 percent of the entire US food supply. Yet alongside this excess of waste, we live in a world of huge inequity, where one in ten people on the planet go hungry every day.

At the heart of these problems is a huge imbalance of power, with a handful of multinational corporations controlling how the majority of food is produced, distributed, and sold. These companies, propped up by unfair trade rules implemented by the World Trade Organization and the International Monetary Fund, prioritise excessive profits over human and animal welfare and result in the exploitative and damaging food system we have today.

So how can we ensure our eating and buying habits support a more just global food system?

Eating more vegetable-based meals is an obvious place to start, with the bonus that it's good for your health too. Supporting local producers, where you can, is another good step, as is buying products that are organic if you can afford to. But while individual action is always a step in the right direction, the radical restructuring of how food is grown, processed, and distributed on the level that is needed for our personal and planetary survival means zooming out to examine the wider forces at play – a rigged global economy, corporate lobbying, our overreliance on fossil fuels, and the continuing pervasive reality of racial injustice. Changing our food system can't be done in isolation but rather will involve a wholesale reorganising of our political economy to meet the very real demands and challenges of the twenty-first century. This should include extending the support we give to farmers, regulating corporate power, protecting local markets, and encouraging fair trade. It's also about boosting the incomes of the most vulnerable people in society so they can afford nutritious food and supporting the rights of migrants, who often can be found toiling in agricultural fields, so they can live and work in dignity.

It that all feels like a tall order, I've got some good news for you. All over the world today there are thousands of incredibly inspiring initiatives, businesses, and social movements working to reshape our food system for the better. You can find them in every town and city, region, and province on the planet – from local farmers' markets to supermarket co-ops, to urban food-growing gardens and organic produce delivery schemes, all the way up to the large social movements such as the MST (Landless Workers' Movement) in Brazil. These networks working outside the corporate food system offer beacons of hope and catalysts for change. In a world where structural change can often feel out of reach or unattainable, engaging with these organisations and movements is a way of adding your actions and purchasing power to the chorus of voices that believe that another food system is possible.

Here are a few of my favourites:

Riverford Organic Farmers (UK)

Founded by radical campaigning farmer Guy Singh-Watson, Riverford is more than a successful organic farm in the West Country of England, it's a pioneering employee-owned enterprise that produces delicious plants, dairy, and meat in sustainable ways while also campaigning against the unjust economic imbalances in our economy and demanding fair farming practices. They also have an incredible restaurant at their HQ that is well worth a visit. **Riverford.co.uk**

Soul Fire Farm (USA)

This community farm in Grafton, upstate New York, promotes food sovereignty as a tool of racial justice and liberation. It uses organic and ancestral regenerative farming techniques to combat injustice in the food system and has become a leading training centre for BIPOC farmers, working to reclaim the narrative around how the right to healthy food is a racial justice issue. **SoulFireFarm.org**

Zaytoun (Palestine)

All over the world, small-scale farmers are under pressure, but there are few places harder to survive than Palestine. This organisation directly supports Palestinian farmers through selling their products such as extra-virgin olive oil, za'atar, and Medjool dates to consumers in the West. I started off buying their products on ethical grounds, but I continue because their products taste so good! **Zaytoun.uk**

Via Campesina (Worldwide)

Arguably the largest social movement in the world, this radical network founded in the Global South is an alliance of small-scale family farmers, farmworkers, rural women's groups, and Indigenous and landless peoples. As of 2020, it had 182 groups in 81 countries and represented around 200 million people fighting for their right to food sovereignty. Its campaigning work has dramatically changed the global conversation about agriculture and corporate control of the food system at the highest level. **ViaCampesina.org**

Acknowledgments

IT TAKES A village to create a book, and I feel incredibly fortunate to have been able to collaborate with some of the top talents in our industry on this one.

From Jonathan Gregson and his vibrant showstopping photography, to Max Robinson's eye-catching prop arrangements and Rosie Reynolds's mouth-watering food styling – I'm so thankful to this photography dream team and so proud of what they created.

The wonderful Catherine Phipps helped me test these recipes – huge thanks for your feedback, shortcuts, and creative contributions.

Thanks to my agent, Kim Witherspoon at Inkwell Management, who, alongside Jessica Mileo at Inkwell, patiently and proactively worked with me across several book proposals. Thanks for your sage advice and words of motivation.

Special thanks to my publishers, W. W. Norton and Bloomsbury UK, with whom I've had the pleasure of working on four books now and who always work so hard to produce and publicise my books. Thanks to Melanie Tortoroli for her support, trust, and belief in me as a writer, something that continues to push me and inspires me to do better. To Allison Chi for her stunning design work and Will Scarlett for his endlessly positive PR enthusiasm – you have all been a dream to work with. Over in the UK, thanks to Rowan Yapp for her wise insights and guidance, Kiron Gill for her easeful, supportive way of working and exceptional eye for detail and Isobel Turton for being a brilliant PR ambassador for the book. Thanks also to Claire Scott for her amazing PR work and Issy Croker for the beautiful author shots. The gorgeous cover design by David Mann brought the book to life and I'm especially grateful for it.

Thanks to my family, in the UK, USA, Iran, and Pakistan. Writing this book made me realise how deeply my everyday home cooking is rooted in my heritage. What a gift that is, and how proud I am, that we have all kept such a strong link to our traditions.

And finally, thanks to Mark, for inspiring so many of these recipes and for helping me create a new family with whom to share the legacy of my ancestors. I hope the scent of saffron, the crunch of tahdig, and the sharp tang of pomegranates fill our kitchen with happiness for many years to come.

Index

Note: Page references in *italics* indicate photographs.

About the Author

Issy Croker

YASMIN KHAN is an award-winning food and travel writer, broadcaster, and human rights activist. Her best-selling cookbooks, *The Saffron Tales*, *Zaitoun*, and *Ripe Figs*, share recipes and stories from the Middle East and Eastern Mediterranean and celebrate the power of the human spirit in places more commonly associated with conflict.

Instagram yasminkhanstories
Substack Risingup.substack.com

BLOOMSBURY PUBLISHING
Bloomsbury Publishing Plc
50 Bedford Square, London, WC1B 3DP, UK
Bloomsbury Publishing Ireland Limited,
29 Earlsfort Terrace, Dublin 2, D02 AY28, Ireland

BLOOMSBURY, BLOOMSBURY PUBLISHING and the Diana logo are trademarks of Bloomsbury Publishing Plc

First published in 2025 in the USA by W. W. Norton & Company, Inc.
First published in Great Britain in 2025

Photos on pages 10 and 247 are by Issy Croker
Book design: Allison Chi
Illustrations: Mariam Tafsiri
Production controller: Laura Brodie

A catalogue record for this book is available from the British Library

HB: 978-1-526-66495-2 eBook: 978-1-526-66496-9

2 4 6 8 10 9 7 5 3 1

Printed in Dubai by Oriental Press

FSC MIX Paper | Supporting responsible forestry FSC® C004800

To find out more about our authors and books visit www.bloomsbury.com and sign up for our newsletters

For product safety related questions contact productsafety@bloomsbury.com